Memoirs of a
BIBLE
SMUGGLER

JEANA KENDRICK

Also By Jeana Kendrick

St. Abient Run

The Paris Conspiracy

The Last Bridge Across Mostar

Memoirs of a
BIBLE
SMUGGLER

JEANA KENDRICK

Northridge Press
Conroe, Texas
2021

Northridge Press

Copyright © 2021 by Jeana Kendrick

USA

Library of Congress cataloging in publication data

Kendrick, Jeana
    Memoirs of a Bible Smuggler / Jeana Kendrick – First Edition
    pages; cm

Cover photos: Jeff Kendrick
Cover design: Tim Barber—Dissect Designs
Book design interior layout: Michael Mayfield

ISBN 978-1-952406-06-5 (Hardback) ISBN 978-1-952406-00-3 (trade paperback)–
ISBN 978-1-952406-02-7 (e-book) – ISBN 978-1-952406-01-0 (audio)

Northridge Press
P.O. Box 2561
Conroe, TX 77305

Printed in the United States of America

To my husband Jeff and my family for their unfailing love and encouragement and to persecuted Christians throughout the world.

Some trust in chariots, and some in horses: but we will remember the name of the Lord our God (Psalms 20:7).

Contents

Acknowledgments

Memoirs of a Bible Smuggler could not have been written without the assistance of a number of people. I would like to offer enormous thanks to my weekly critique friends and authors, Jacqueline Pelham, Beverly Butt and Joy Zeigler who shared their editorial insights and have inspired me year after year. A special thank you to my dear friend, mentor and author extraordinaire Guida Jackson, Rita Mills, my sister Kathryn Kendrick, and family and friends for their encouragement and support. Thanks also to the persecuted pastors and their families, Bible couriers and many others we've worked with at Door of Hope International, especially Paul Popov, Ivette Moradian and Ruth Shevchenko. Any mistakes or errors are my own. Lastly, thanks to my husband Jeff who makes it all possible and has helped and cheered me on throughout this endeavor.

1

Trouble at the Russian Border

Summer 1983

MY HUSBAND JEFF AND I were rapidly approaching the Soviet border when a teammate slipped a tiny one-by-two-inch tape recorder into the palm of my hand.

Shelly's usually bright face was clouded, and her mouth turned down in apology. "Sorry. Back in Austria, Paul asked me to give you this."

My gaze darted about the van. It was too late to create a hiding place the officials wouldn't find. I dropped the mini recorder into my purse and whispered, "God we need a miracle." Though this was our third year as Bible smugglers, crossing into Communist countries was still frightening.

Earlier that week in Austria, we'd attended a Door of Hope International (DOHI) board meeting with mission president, Paul Popov. I knew the tapes from the meeting could incriminate us and feared Shelly had unknowingly handed one of them to me.

The van came to a halt and the Soviet officers initiated the search rituals I recognized too well. They slid beneath the van to check the undercarriage, took the doors apart and removed the wheels to X-ray the tires.

The officers demanded to see our passports and luggage. Finally, one turned to me and said, "Give me your purse."

Panicked, images of what could happen flashed across my mind. Adrenaline surged through me. The recorder could expose not only the passengers in our van but also the two DOHI teams being searched several lanes over, whom we pretended not to know.

I struggled to keep my expression blank to conceal my alarm and handed my purse to the officer as if I had nothing to hide.

He pulled out my wallet and a packet of tissues, tossing them aside. A triumphant gleam lit his eyes as he grasped the mini recorder and held it up. "What's this?"

I smiled, striving to keep the tremor from my voice. "A recorder, for music or whatever." My prayers raced heavenward: Lord, we've been in tight situations before and by Your grace miraculously escaped time and time again. Please, safeguard us now.

The officer pushed the Play button and as Paul Popov's Swedish-accented English rumbled forth, I reflected on how we had landed in this fix, thousands of miles from our Texas home, in the middle of a Cold War.

In 1980, when my husband Jeff and I initially embarked on these missions, we were incredibly young and idealistic. There was a sense of being part of something immensely beyond ourselves. We were lured by the thrill of driving on dark winding roads in vehicles loaded with Bibles that our faithful brothers and sisters eagerly awaited. The plight of these Christians in Communist countries who were willing to sacrifice their lives for Bibles inspired us. Yet with each passing year our vulnerability and chances of being arrested increased.

Before ever traveling to Eastern Europe, we had prayerfully and financially assisted missions for years, devouring books and reports that told of the suffering behind the Iron Curtain. The more we learned, the deeper our burden grew until eventually we were led to serve overseas. Clueless about how to begin, Jeff and I wondered if it might be an impossible dream.

Then we happened to read a David Wilkerson book, detailing how God inspired him to spend an extra hour each evening in prayer. The outgrowth of his prayer was the well-known ministry Teen Challenge. Jeff and I followed his example and amazingly, within a matter of months we were in Eastern Europe, smuggling thousands of Bibles behind the Iron Curtain via the ministry of Door of Hope International.

We learned of DOHI's ministry to persecuted Christians through its founder Haralan Popov's autobiography, *Tortured For His Faith*. From 1937 to 1946, he pastored the church in Burgas, which grew to be the largest protestant church in Bulgaria. Haralan then moved to Sofia as overseer of church planting and evangelism for the entire country. In 1948, the Communists arrested the country's leading ministers including Haralan, alleging they were US spies. They held a mock trial and sentenced fifteen pastors to prison. Haralan's wife Ruth and their two small children, Rhoda and Paul, were left with no financial support while he served more than thirteen years in the gulag.

On Bulgaria's Belene Island, his prison barracks were huts made of willow branches that housed six thousand inmates. Only a few hundred survived. It was a miracle that Haralan lived through the eighteen-hour days of hard labor in the freezing cold during the harsh winter months, with almost no food and very little clothing for protection.

After Haralan was released from prison in September 1961, he joined his wife and children who had left Bulgaria and were now in Sweden, bringing with him a commission from those he left behind. "Please," they pleaded, "bring us Bibles, for we have none." Initially, Haralan worked with Slaviska Mission in Stockholm for several years. Then, with the support of friends, he founded an organization that translated, printed and distributed Bibles as well as Christian literature and humanitarian aid in Eastern Europe during a period when many had forgotten the millions persecuted behind the Iron Curtain.

Now, as Jeff and I stood on the Soviet border with Haralan's son, Paul Popov's voice booming from the recorder, I prayed for God's grace and courage.

I thought of Raoul Wallenberg, the Swedish diplomat who saved tens of thousands of Hungarian Jews during World War II. When asked about the risk to himself, he said, it was not often a man was given such an opportunity to act, maybe once in a lifetime.

His words echoed in my mind as the Soviet officer played the mini recorder. I glanced nonchalantly toward Jeff, knowing he, too, was praying for divine intervention.

2

Expectations

I STILL MARVEL at how we came to be involved. After Jeff and I followed the Holy Spirit's leading, setting aside extra time for daily prayer, our lives started to change. One afternoon I opened the mail and found a newsletter with a plea for volunteers to smuggle Bibles. That evening, I gave Jeff the letter to read. "Can you imagine us bringing Bibles to the Christians we've been praying for?"

Jeff smiled at my enthusiasm, his blue eyes gentle. "We can't afford to simply quit our jobs and travel overseas. As much as we might like to, it's not practical." His arms slipped around me.

At six-feet-four, he towered over me as I ruffled his red hair, then rested my forehead against his chest. "We can pray about it and if it's God's will, He'll provide."

"Okay. And let's be thankful we have enough money to help support Christians in need and can share their stories with others in our area."

I agreed yet continued to pray. I even confided my desire to be a Bible Smuggler to my neighbor and friend, Diane Burnich. For years on our daily two-mile walks, we had shared our hopes and worries. As we wound our way around the block, Diane looked at me curiously. More than likely, she thought I was air dreaming. Eastern Europe seemed light years away from the East Texas piney woods surrounding us.

Our desire to do more for persecuted believers continued to grow. Jeff and I prayed and left the matter entirely in God's hands, taking no other measures to accomplish the goal. Interestingly, a small magazine

Jeff occasionally wrote for requested an article on organizations serving Christians behind the Iron Curtain. The two of us caught a flight to Los Angeles where we visited Brother Andrew's Open Doors, Corrie Ten Boom's mission and others. Jeff interviewed people we had previously only read about, such as Michael Wurmbrant with Jesus to the Communist World, and Paul H. Popov with Door of Hope International.

Paul, whom we came to know as a visionary, spoke softly in a Swedish-Bulgarian accent. His earnest enthusiasm, handsome boyish face and huge brown eyes drew us. But his vast knowledge and grasp of governments and their impact on believers worldwide wowed us.

When he learned Jeff owned a construction company, he pressed us. "Fill out applications. The mission needs volunteers to do major remodeling on the Austrian base."

Jeff appeared dubious. "Wouldn't it be a lot easier to hire carpenters there?"

"Less than five percent of the population is evangelical," Paul said. "Considering the secret nature of the mission, it would be difficult to find local people to work."

After some discussion, Jeff accepted the application forms but cautioned, "I doubt much will come of this. It's simply too hard for us to get away."

Back at home, I mailed the applications as promised. Yet it came as a surprise one night in March of 1980, while our home was filled with guests, to receive Paul's call. "You have both been accepted as missionaries with Door of Hope International and will be stationed in Austria. We would like you to arrive there in April and spend the entire summer working at the courier base. How soon can you leave?"

Thrilled to be invited and longing to go, we realized it would be impossible to come at this time. Since we were self-employed, April 15 generally brought a hefty tax bill, and it was usually August before we managed to pay it down. We explained this to Paul.

"What if you earned enough money to pay your taxes early?" Paul asked.

The conversation went on and eventually Jeff agreed, "If we can take care of Uncle Sam in time, we'll be glad to come." Neither of us imagined this would happen. Perhaps our conversation was a foreshadowing of what was to occur. In the years ahead, Paul became the impetus behind many of our impromptu trips. I recall one occasion in West Berlin when he catapulted us into leading a Soviet ministry trip. Within the hour we found ourselves dashing to East Germany to catch a flight to Moscow.

Back to that night in Conroe, after we hung up with Paul we prayed and before we knew it, tax day rolled around, and somehow, we had earned more money than expected.

Jeff phoned Paul. "We can hardly believe it. Our taxes are paid, and Jeana and I are able to commit to three months overseas helping out."

"The evening I asked you to come," Paul confided, "I was sitting in my office studying missionary applications. When I read yours, I had a good feeling about you both. I looked across at one of the staff and said, 'These two are just the people we need.' I picked up the phone and dialed your number."

Awestruck at how God was moving in our lives, we somehow managed a response.

Paul continued. "Regarding this summer, you'll need some instruction, and unfortunately, you have missed DOHI's annual missionary training seminar. Is your home large enough to accommodate several of our staff for four or five days while they brief and prepare you for the ministry ahead?"

Elated by how quickly events were evolving, I rushed to say, "We've plenty of space and would love to have them here."

Before long, Maria, a tall brunette with a warm smile who was the mission's European director; Dee Dee, a sparkling blonde missionary with DOHI/Sweden; Grace and Kathy, who headed DOHI's base in Thessaloniki, Greece; and Richard, another new recruit from Texas, arrived at our Conroe home for a four-day training session.

The group shared stories of secret missions and rendezvous with

Christians behind the Iron Curtain that sounded like fiction thrillers. They related experiences of near mishaps and told in breathtaking detail how repeatedly they were miraculously delivered from the hands of their oppressors, generally the Communist authorities.

They also warned, mission funds were tight, because the need was so great. Missionaries were often compelled to dip into their personal funds to cover costs, and although DOHI could be counted on to reimburse them, the lag time could be lengthy.

We were given a whirlwind crash course in mission policy, Eastern European church etiquette, missionary dress code, border crossings, navigation, base management and Bible smuggling.

For meals, everyone gathered in our large blue and yellow country kitchen. I enjoyed cooking and had prepared the evening meals ahead. For breakfast we ate my homemade granola or whole wheat pancakes and for lunch I served sandwiches. Maria declared that I would be a great asset at the base because of my ease in handling groups. Little did I know then how prophetic her words were to be.

And little did I dream that one day I would face a glaring Soviet officer who held the fate of our team in his hands.

3

A Rough Landing

IN APRIL 1980, Jeff and I flew into Frankfurt on our first overseas mission trip. Richard picked us up at the airport and stuffed our luggage and me into the back of a Volkswagen Beetle already crammed high with boxes of files and equipment. The two men climbed into the front, and we commenced the ten-hour journey to DOHI's Austrian base. At the Continental Divide in Germany, we paused to snap photos of Jeff and me, sheltered beneath the breathtaking cascade of mountains.

When at last we reached the city of Spittal an der Drau, I decompressed my jet-lagged body, scrambling from the back seat onto a faintly lit parking lot. The three of us gazed at the gray stucco two-story courier base sequestered beneath the Alps. The dark purple silhouette of Goldeck Mountain appeared close enough to touch. A beacon light crowned its snow-capped height.

Maria's assistant, Mark Abrams, came out of the adjacent three-story Swedish Alliance Mission where he was staying. He welcomed us. "I must apologize, no one has made any advance arrangements for your lodging."

Jeff and I smiled uncertainly, shaking hands with him.

Mark continued. "Pastor Alexander Ferrari and his wife Erna who head the Swedish mission outreach said you can stay there tonight. Tomorrow you'll need to find another place."

I exchanged a bewildered glance with Jeff. What were we going to do? We didn't have funds to live indefinitely at a hotel in an expensive tourist spot.

"I understood from Paul and Maria we were to live at the base," Jeff said.

9

"As you'll soon see," Mark said, "it's not yet habitable. Richard, you can bunk with me." He led us inside the DOHI courier base, leaving the starry evening behind. The upstairs kitchen, dining room and offices were in a state of total disrepair, distinguished by multi-layers of peeling paint, wallpaper and mold. The basement living quarters had dirt floors.

The old bread factory's redeeming feature was the four double garages in good working order. The ceilings were fourteen feet high and each of the garages measured about forty-by-forty-feet. However, the vehicles within were in need of some repair.

Far from daunted, Jeff and I were eager to whip the place into shape. We unloaded our gear and walked around to Pastor Alexander's establishment, unsure what we would encounter.

His daughter gave us a measured look, then led us to the room next to Mark's and unlocked the door. "This is for tonight only. Our Swedish youth teams will be arriving and need this space." As if to press the point, she reiterated, "You must be gone by tomorrow."

My heart sank at her words. Neither Jeff nor I could understand why DOHI had failed to make the promised arrangements. They must have believed the base was in much better condition than it was.

We soon learned Pastor Alexander Ferrari and his petite brunette wife Erna had been prominent Nazis during World War II. While stationed in Stockholm, they became born-again Christians through the evangelical outreach of Swedish Alliance Mission. After the war, supported by the same organization, he returned to Austria as a pastor with his family and set up a church and mission to evangelize Spittal. Swedish teams arrived intermittently throughout the year to assist in these efforts. A popular book based on Alexander's dramatic conversion, left him much in demand as a conference speaker across Europe.

At the time as beautiful as it was, Spittal had a high suicide rate. In the late '80s, the town elected the first mayor who had not been a member of the Nazi party. It was a difficult field for missionaries. We heard that many couples who came to the area for ministry purposes ended up divorcing due to the strain.

Alex and Erna had the advantage of being Spittal natives. In his sixties, Alex was tall, robust and fair with laughing eyes. He often joked that his wife kept him in line. Eventually, we became the best of friends, but during our first month there, under pressure because he was expecting the Swedes, Alex tried to oust us, daily, as politely as he could. Much to our benefit, the Swedish youth were continually delayed.

Austria was also experiencing its coldest spring in fifteen years. We looked at the snow-covered mountains surrounding Spittal and hung on to our room at Alex's, knowing we couldn't sleep in the garages and apartment next door without freezing.

In our mid-thirties and accustomed to some measure of control and respect, we found it humbling to be stranded and dependent on the reluctant help of strangers. Despite a severe case of homesickness, I resisted the temptation to pack up and fly back to the US. We'd made a commitment. Still, I counted the days until our departure.

One morning while washing the breakfast dishes, Mark and I fell into a discussion about the willingness of Christians to go wherever God called.

Without thinking it through I said, "I'd be willing to go anywhere God wants me."

Mark appeared skeptical. "Would you? Even if it was to stay here permanently?"

His question startled me, and I struggled to give an honest answer. It was clear to everyone, I missed Texas and couldn't wait to leave.

Finally, I nodded. "Even here. Though I hope it's not what He wants." Reflecting on our conversation, it revealed a portent of what the Lord had in store. He didn't require me to be ready at that moment to make a big leap of faith, only willing. He took care of the rest and gave me the heart to stay.

4

Answered Prayer

SINCE NEITHER JEFF NOR I SPOKE German then, we depended on Mark, pocket dictionaries and phrase books to get by. Our room was large and pleasant, yet I chuckle to think of the king-size bed made with two sets of flat twin sheets. We awoke each morning to a tangled mess. When I inquired about fitted sheets, the salesclerks shook their heads at the absurdity. Only twin-sized flat sheets were sold. When it was cold, Austrian husbands and wives could each curl up in their own sheets and duvet-covered down comforters.

The locals turned the heat off in the day and set it on high for the night, the reverse of what we did at home. After enduring the biting cold throughout the day, we would lie awake at night in the stifling heat, too hot to sleep.

In the mornings, we'd stumble into the kitchen where a group of Austrians, eating oatmeal, would greet us in unison, *"Guten Morgen."* For weeks I daydreamed of how pleasant it would be to hear a soft, melodious, "Good morning."

Our days were spent working at the DOHI base next door. With Mark and Richard's help, Jeff poured concrete floors in the basement, built bunk beds, laid tile floors and showers and constructed kitchen cabinets upstairs.

Meanwhile, I sewed curtains for the windows and tracked down furnishings and supplies at bargain prices. I tackled the RVs as well, fashioning new cushion and window coverings. Every day was an adventure while shopping with my dictionary and my small but growing vocabulary.

Members of Alex's church helped, especially Anita, a petite, blond dynamo, and her soft-spoken husband Walter who was fluent in English. Anita's English was limited to broken phrases.

The afternoon we met, she rode her bicycle to the base where we were working. A smile lighting her elfish face, she said, "I—Anita—speak only—little English." Her brown eyes dancing, she pointed to me. "I—your friend. What—is—your—name?"

Delighted, I said, "Jeana."

We studied each other, two young women happy with what we saw. "You come my house for coffee," she said.

I nodded. "*Danke.*"

She pushed her bike, walking alongside me on the ten-minute trek to her home.

A shortcut through the town's flour mill led us down steep stone steps and across a short wooden bridge. Anita motioned toward the huge wooden wheels harnessing the river's power to grind the grains. She said, "*Müller.*"

At her request, I struggled to pronounce their word for miller, and she broke into peels of infectious laughter. She kept repeating the *ü* sound, giggling at my attempts to mimic her.

Anita lived in a neighborhood of attractive two-story dwellings with manicured lawns. Red and pink geraniums peeked from window boxes, and small orchards and gardens edged the backyards. Inside each abode, four families resided. Anita's parents, who owned half of one house, lived downstairs, and Anita, her husband Walter and their teenage son, Deiter, upstairs.

What a warm welcome I received. Her parents were introduced as simply *Oma* and *Opa* or as we say, Grandma and Granddad. Walter who was eager to practice his English translated. He said that from her youth, Anita had yearned to have an American friend and was delighted to have found me.

Oma served her marvelous homemade apple strudel with mounds of whipped cream. We drank freshly ground, brewed coffee, swirled with whipped cream as well. Until then, I hadn't cared for coffee, but I have been a devotee ever since.

While we ate, Anita told her family about our walk there. Still chuckling, she pointed to the refrigerator and said, "*Kühlschrank.*" I recognized my cue and as expected, my bumbling attempts to say the *ü* sound afforded them great entertainment.

The next week she arranged for her cousin who taught English to give Jeff and me German lessons. I learned the *ou* sound in Houston was equivalent to their *ü* sound.

Walter often translated for Jeff when he purchased supplies for the remodeling project. Anita also helped me shop for the base. At the grocery store, she would motion to items she thought we could use and pantomime their contents. On one occasion, she paused next to a row of wine-shaped bottles with apples on the label. Anita brought her fingers to her lips in a kissing motion. "Mmm."

I put the bottle in my cart, believing it to be apple juice, and then stopped at the meat counter to order a chicken. Back at the base, I placed both in the refrigerator. The next afternoon I poured myself a glass of juice and brought out the package of chicken wrapped in butcher paper.

I swallowed a large gulp of the juice and choked, realizing with a shudder it was apple cider vinegar. Then I unwrapped the chicken and stared aghast at the attached head and feet, and still intact innards. That night the men dressed the chicken for supper.

Several evenings later, we attended a Full Gospel Businessmen's dinner at a nearby hotel. Jeff and I sat in the banquet area with Anita, Walter and the wife of Franz, the association president. Naively, I ordered ice water from one of the waiters scurrying to and fro taking orders and delivering drinks to the various attendees.

When it never came, I reordered. Meanwhile, Anita kept staring at me and flapping her arms and clucking like a chicken, saying, "*Hühn, Hühn.*"

I was at a loss until they served us chicken. I then realized she had been trying to tell me what we were having for dinner.

That settled, I took the opportunity to ask the waiter once more for ice water.

Anita intervened in her delightfully accented broken English. "*Bitte*, bring her *das ice wasser*. My friend is an American. She does not understand."

He nodded and left.

I wondered why ordering ice water should be so difficult. At the head table, Franz rose to address the crowd just as our waiter, bearing a tray with a large glass pitcher of iced water, and several glasses, crossed the entire length of the dining room.

The crowd's attention was caught.

Franz paused and the room seemed to hold its breath. When the waiter set the tray in front of Jeff and me, everyone's gaze was riveted. Those seated nearby seemed to shrivel in embarrassment.

Franz greeted the group, shifting the focus from us.

With the crisis apparently averted, Jeff lifted the pitcher and poured. The subsequent clunk—as ice plopped into the glasses echoed across the vast room. Every gaze appeared to, again, turn our way.

Franz's wife looked as if she wished to disappear. Eventually everyone's attention was caught up in the ongoing program and Jeff and I quietly sipped our water.

Franz's wife unwittingly reached for one of the glasses and poured herself a drink. The clunk-clunk of the ice drew the crowd's regard back to our table. Franz's wife never took a sip of her water. And Jeff and I learned never to request ice. Mineral water, which is priced by the glass, is the preferred drink.

In Spittal, the remodeling was eventually completed. Richard, Mark, Jeff and I moved into the Door of Hope International base to prepare for the summer's teams.

A few weeks later Jeff walked into the kitchen. "There's been a glitch," he said. "Paul has asked us to drive an RV loaded with Bibles into Hungary, Romania and Bulgaria. The couriers scheduled to rendezvous with Paul and Maria can't come."

I felt like dancing, yet all I could say was, "Wow."

Every night since our arrival, I had prayed God would send us to Romania or Bulgaria. I wanted to meet the persecuted brethren we prayed for daily. God had answered my prayer and I was beyond excited.

5

Reality Came Knocking

BY DAY, IN THE HUGE MISSION garages, the men loaded Bibles into the 1975 white Ford pickup camper's secret compartments and performed mechanical feats I am at a loss to describe. Meanwhile, I shopped and packed for the trip East.

In the evenings, we sat in the makeshift office we'd created, while Mark briefed Jeff and me in preparation for our departure. Against my will, my gaze wandered to the barely visible mold spreading beneath the wallpaper, wishing for the opportunity and funds to redo it. Still, I listened intently as Mark discussed border crossings, rendezvous details, meetings with Christians and the routes we would travel.

Mark said, "The plan is for you to drive to Vienna, get visas and then proceed to Hungary. Their border station is large and sophisticated. Customs should be easy. Hungary doesn't want to discourage its tourist business."

Jeff shifted thoughtfully in the hard wooden chair. "So there's no need to worry about the Bibles getting through Hungary?"

"Busts have been known to occur, but they're infrequent. Romania's inspections will be much more arduous and could last seven to eight hours."

We nodded in understanding. Jeff and I had read reports on Romania's Communist regime and knew they routinely violated human rights, persecuting Christians.

Mark handed us a list of addresses. "Memorize these and destroy them before you leave Austria. In Budapest, Hungary, you're to deliver Bibles at the corresponding address to Lazlo and his wife. Make it late at night to avoid detection. Once you're in the country, wear rubber-soled shoes to deflect noise and dark clothing that'll blend with the natives' attire."

Already I could see I'd need to run out and buy a few more outfits before we left. I had no idea how the natives dressed. "Is the long jean skirt I'm wearing okay?"

Mark shook his head. "You shouldn't look too Christian or conservative at the border, just touristy."

"I'm confused. Which is it? Do you want us to dress like tourists or natives?"

"At the borders you want to appear like naive tourists who are traveling to enjoy the scenery and sights. Inside the country, avoid drawing attention to yourselves by dressing like the natives. The last thing you want to do is stand out when you're delivering Bibles at night."

"That makes sense."

He continued. "Your next stop will be Romania, one of the most difficult borders to cross. Maria will be driving the Volvo from Germany to Bucharest. Paul will arrive in Arad and you'll rendezvous at the train station. Follow his lead. As the mission's VP and European director, Paul and Maria are high-profile. They can't be seen with you or near the Bibles. To do so could risk the entire operation."

I felt the thrill of a new galaxy opening to us, yet a few questions remained. "What if the border guards ask if we have Bibles?"

Mark stared at me in consternation. "I can't believe you're asking me this now. You can't tell them you have Bibles." He rested his head in his hands for a moment. "Didn't they teach you anything?"

The mere suggestion of our possibly lying rocked me. I gazed at Mark, appalled. "I never thought we'd be expected to lie."

He groaned at my naivety. "An alternative is to declare the Bibles, then stand by and watch them confiscate every book. What did you think was going to happen?"

"Certainly not this."

My concern mirrored in Jeff's eyes, he said, "You're going to have to explain this to us. To lie goes against everything we believe."

Mark challenged, "Rahab the harlot lied, and God rewarded her for it."

Jeff and I exchanged searching glances.

"When you reach the Romanian border, customs will ask if you have Bibles. You have two options: tell them the truth or lie. You better think hard about what you are going to say." Mark picked up a book and several pamphlets from the newly installed shelves and gave them to Jeff. "These are required reading for DOHI missionaries. I don't know how you guys slipped through the cracks."

Jeff accepted the materials. "All we can do is read these and pray about it."

Enlightenment didn't come overnight, dazzling us with its brilliance. We had bypassed DOHI's customary missionary training, our initial task being to oversee the remodeling of the Austrian base.

Mark understood the truth could endanger those Christians we sought to help and might lead to revealing their involvement, including names and addresses. Also, DOHI was not a wealthy mission and couldn't afford to have its vehicles confiscated.

The Bibles were not an issue as they were too valuable a commodity to be destroyed. Border guards oftentimes sold them on the black market. Sadly, on one occasion Romanian authorities opened a Christian Bookstore using the seized Bibles, as a ploy to ferret out and arrest practicing Christians.

Our safety wasn't the preeminent concern. Generally, if caught, couriers were arrested and interrogated for a few days, then released. In Czechoslovakia, they would be sentenced to serve mandatory prison terms. More than official arrests, couriers feared possible disappearances. There were rumors about people who had simply vanished and about those who, by the grace of God, managed to escape years later.

As a Christian, I had never contemplated lying. According to Revelations 21:8, "all liars shall have their part in the lake which burneth with fire and brimstone: which is the second death." I didn't even believe in white lies.

A crash course in the ethics of Bible smuggling ensued. In the Old Testament, Rahab the Harlot hid two Israelite spies in Jericho and lied when the king asked her where they were. For this act of bravery, she and her family were spared when the Israelites seized control of the land (Josh. 2:6). Rahab is also listed with many great men of faith in the New Testament: "By faith the harlot Rahab perished not with them that believed not, when she had received the spies with peace," (Heb. 11:31).

In the ensuing years, whenever Jeff and I spoke to churches about Door of Hope International's ministry, regardless of the country, someone in the audience invariably posed the question, "What if they ask if you have Bibles?"

The audience would murmur, shocked that two seemingly dedicated missionaries condoned lying. It was rough ground and we covered it as fast as possible to prevent an outbreak of division.

I certainly don't condone lying but wouldn't hesitate to do so if necessary in similar circumstances. It is not difficult for me to reconcile the Scriptures in Hebrews and Joshua with those in Revelations. It was not sinful for Jesus to pluck corn on the Sabbath when He and His disciples were hungry. God's law was made for man and not the reverse.

Some major denominations refused to concede this principle, and in so doing, denied assistance to persecuted and oppressed Christians under Communist regimes in Eastern Europe. Some also shunned organizations such as Door of Hope International because they *broke the law* by smuggling Bibles. After the Iron Curtain fell, many of these same organizations and denominations began active ministries to those in need in these countries.

Jeff and I accompanied Haralan and Paul in the mid '80s to the Zurich World Pentecostal Conference. On this momentous occasion, the

Assemblies of God foreign mission's director conceded after twenty-five years that they had been wrong on this issue and asked Haralan's forgiveness. This meant so much to Haralan.

I also remember attending Sunday worship services at the American embassy in Moscow. We had Bibles and hymn books within those *sacred walls* while without, people were beaten and imprisoned, because they wanted a Bible. Still, the Americans there with whom I spoke, believed it would be wrong for them to break the law by sharing their Bibles.

At this time, the US ambassador to Romania, David B. Funderburk, was noted for helping Christians. He protested our government's policy of granting Most Favored Nation status to Romania despite their continued abuse of human rights.

Christians were being persecuted for their faith in Romania and other Communist countries, in spite of their constitutions granting them religious liberties, which the controlling authorities chose not to honor.

Fortunately, while many major denominations condemned Bible smuggling, their individual congregations around the world supported it, enabling DOHI to deliver more than a million Bibles as well as other Christian literature and humanitarian aid when it was desperately needed.

I always thought of it as the Esther question—this great difference between East and West. King Ahasuerus, who reigned over more than one hundred twenty-seven provinces from Ethiopia to India, chose Esther, a Jewish handmaiden, to be his queen. Now it so happened the king promoted Haman, who sought to destroy the Jews. Thus, at a period when the queen lived in great prosperity, her people were in great peril. Mordecai, her uncle, sent her a message, "Think not within thyself that thou shalt escape in the king's house, more than all the Jews . . . and who knoweth whether thou art come to the kingdom for such a time as this," (Esther 4:13, 14).

By the law of the land, the queen could be put to death for approaching the king without an invitation. Still Esther sent a message to Mordecai, requesting all of the Jews to join her and her handmaidens in fasting. After they had prayed and fasted for three days, she approached King Ahasuerus, believing God had placed her in a place of prosperity and responsibility for that very purpose. Thus, Esther saved her people.

In like manner, we as Christians are urged to help if we see a brother or sister in need. The book of Hebrews admonishes us to, "Remember those in bonds as though bound with them."

6

Eastward Bound

ONE SUMMER MORNING IN 1980, after group prayer and lots of hugs and wishes for a fruitful trip, Jeff and I left. We traveled north on the autobahn, enjoying the lush green Alps sprinkled with crystal blue lakes and pristine church spires rising above villages centuries old.

On the four to five-hour journey to Vienna, we memorized the addresses of the places where we were to rendezvous with Paul, Maria and other contacts. When we reached Vienna, Jeff drove downtown, circling the inner ring for a parking spot. This wasn't easy to find for a vehicle the size of the camper.

I gazed raptly at the opulent Vienna State Opera, Max's Theater Café, Saint Stephen's Cathedral and other engaging sights until Jeff reminded me I was supposed to be navigating, which meant observing the street signs and the map rather than sightseeing.

Somehow we managed to park, despite the police directing everyone away and the delivery trucks hogging any spaces left from the swarm of cars streaming in and out. Horses, carriages, pedestrians and bicyclers further congested the area.

We strolled along the busy main street in search of the embassies, glimpsing Vienna's famous walk plaza, a shopping area where artists performed songs, dances, and skits. On the corner, a small vendor was selling tempting European burgers sandwiched between hard rolls and mustard, but we were in too much of a hurry to stop and eat.

It was a magical scene certain to light this country girl's imagination.

To think, I was in Vienna where dignitaries in the 1700s negotiated the end of the Napoleonic war; the city Soviet troops controlled in part for a decade following World War II. Vienna was the golden metropolis where Strauss first introduced the waltz, and where we were told three hundred missionaries to Eastern Europe now lived, perhaps side-by-side with Communist spies.

On most any other occasion, it would have been pleasant to stop at one of the *Konditoreis* for *Apfelstrudel* and coffee. I would have also enjoyed browsing in the elegant shops lining *Stephansplatz*, a walk plaza in Vienna's center named after the nearby *Stephansdom*. Instead, we visited the Hungarian, Romanian, and Bulgarian embassies to obtain the required visas before they closed. After hours of filling out forms in duplicate, taking lots of photos and waiting in lines, we purchased our visas.

In the late afternoon, we finally headed for the Hungarian border. I can't think of a time when we've been more excited. Soon we would be meeting Christian brothers and sisters in Eastern Europe and giving them Bibles.

A spring sun shone through the windshield, speckling my face and arms as I felt the gray chill of the East Bloc, the stark atmosphere drawing us into its vortex, ostensibly vanquishing Vienna's gaiety and glamour. There were no chatty tourists strolling past or flowers blooming in pretty window boxes. The architecture seemed colder, stripped of the majestic artistry so often integral to Austria's charm. Unfinished buildings of fluted red cinder block and mortar lined the streets. I received the impression of shutters tightly drawn and a city in hiding.

About thirty minutes before we reached Hungary, Jeff pulled the camper to the side of the road and turned off the engine. "Give me the addresses," he said.

With a furtive glance to ensure no one was watching, I reached into my blouse, pulled out the now memorized contacts and handed them to Jeff. My heart thumped wildly as I observed the area beyond the passenger side of the truck cab, fearing we looked too suspicious. He held the list with one hand and struck a match with the other, setting the papers on fire. We watched them curl and burn, then I rolled down my window, and Jeff leaned across and discreetly threw the ashen conical heap outside.

Finally, we climbed out of the vehicle into the strangeness of the street and initiated a last check of the pickup and camper to guarantee nothing would give us away. Then we got back in the truck, where the road before us seemed to narrow, the faded red buildings closing in, shutting out choices, leading nowhere but East.

7

Hungary

AT TWILIGHT WE ARRIVED at the Hungarian border and parked the camper in one of the glossy-white covered ports. Austrians in Mercedes and BMWs filled most of the berths, opening their car doors, trunks and luggage for official scrutiny.

A customs official stepped up to the truck cab.

Jeff rolled his window down, unable to grasp the torrent of Hungarian the officer spoke. "*Sprechen Sie Englisch?*" Jeff asked.

"*Nein, Deutsch.*" The man held out his hand. "*Ihren Paß, bitte.*"

We presented our passports.

The officer grunted in satisfaction, flipping through the small navy booklets to the pictures, matching our faces to the photos. "*Ah, amerikanische von Texas,*" he said, before paging to the visas stamped at the back. "*Haben Sie etwas zu verzollen?*"

We had learned enough in our language classes with Anita's cousin to reply in German. "No, we've nothing to declare."

"*Hieraus, bitte,*" he ordered.

As we stepped onto the asphalt, he motioned to the team of officers waiting to descend on us. They questioned us, while giving the vehicle an intense search. "*Wo reisen Sie?*"

I tried for a touristy smile. "We're going to Budapest, then on to see as much of Europe as possible while we're on vacation."

"*Wie lange bleiben Sie hier?*"

"It depends on how we feel, a few days, maybe."

Meanwhile, the swarm of agents opened the truck and camper doors, digging through the glove box, as well as behind and under the seats. They examined the doors, the camper cabinets, walls, ceilings, floors and the spaces inside and outside, including underneath.

We hovered nearby, silently petitioning heaven while striving to appear carefree. Mark had warned us not to let our guard down. In an instant, a routine border search could become disastrous.

An official turned to us. *"Öffnen Sie diese Tasche."*

Jeff opened the luggage and the men sifted through our personal belongings.

"Haben Sie noch mehr Gepäck?"

Jeff pointed to the bags. "These are all the suitcases we have."

It took about an hour but permission to enter Hungary was granted. We were eager for our first rendezvous with the Christians. Richard was to meet us covertly at the campground to help dismantle the compartments and package the Hungarian Bibles for delivery later in the evening.

We drove the 171 kilometers to Budapest, down Highway 5, passing through mostly dark, sparsely populated villages until we reached the larger city of Gyor. There streetlamps lit the redbrick storefronts lining the wide boulevard through town. Old men and young shift-workers, dressed in Communist blue, crouched against the buildings to roll a smoke or chat. Hundreds of filled bicycle racks were spaced at frequent intervals along the sidewalks. Dozens more men in blue rode bicycles on the street alongside us.

Beyond Gyor, we took M1 to Budapest. The city was divided into the historical Buda district west of the Danube and the more commercial Pest district east of the river. Jeff drove through Pest's crumbling residential area to an outlying campground on a hill. I hoped there would be an opportunity for us to cross into the more beautiful and ornate Buda for a brief visit.

It was close to ten o'clock when we settled the camper as far back and out of the way as possible. East Europeans vacationing in red, green, orange and blue tents were squeezed into tiny sites like colorful peppers in a jar, up and down the terraced hillside. Some stood by their cars and shelters, changing clothes with a lack of modesty that seemed common in Europe.

Jeff was taking the cabinets apart, when a knock at the door startled us. If the militia walked in and saw the Bibles hidden in the ceiling, we would be arrested. "Who is it?" Jeff called out tensely.

"It's me, Richard."

Relief washed over us, and I hastened to let him in. Richard's eyes widened as he took in the situation, and then he set to work. While the men unloaded and packaged the Bibles, I made sandwiches. When they finished, we ate dinner. Then we prayed and Richard left for the train station to return to the Austrian base. At this stage we were not employing the safer delivery system of using two vehicles. Still, God gave us grace.

An annoying twitch had developed in my right eye. Dressed in dark clothes to blend into the night, and wearing rubber-soled shoes, Jeff and I drove the camper to an outlying rural green stucco home.

Pastor Lazlo, who had been shielded from view by the shrubs, rushed to open the courtyard gate and motioned for us to drive around back, out of sight.

We parked and tiptoed inside, immediately swept into the kitchen by a rather short and wiry Lazlo, and his petite redheaded wife, Maria. They embraced us, then urged us to have a seat around the Formica table.

I was glad they spoke English. It gave us the opportunity to question them about the Hungarian churches' most urgent needs. Their eyes lit up at knowing others cared. They stressed the need for children's materials.

After a while Pastor Lazlo and Jeff unloaded the literature we'd brought.

At the sight of the Bibles, Maria stretched her arms to the heavens. "Thank you, Lord, for bringing my people Your Word."

We regrouped around the table and she said, "Our country was not always Communist. Once we were free to serve God without fear. Hungarians did not want the Soviets to remain after the Second World War." She pointed to Lazlo. "He and our countrymen fought to throw them out.

They held the Soviet army back for four entire days." She spoke with a proud wistfulness of the 1956 Uprising as if it had happened yesterday. "Every man, woman and child among us prayed the West would intervene." She looked at her husband, and shared past sorrow seemed to hum between them like the sad refrain of an old ballad.

Lazlo said, "Help never came. No one wanted to risk a Third World War. They'd just fought two."

"The Soviets put my husband and many others in prison," Maria said. "Such a harsh period for us all."

Jeff and I fumbled for words, yearning in vain to rectify injustices. Maria and Lazlo weren't angling for sympathy or pity, but an acknowledgment and understanding of what their people had endured, both individually and collectively.

With a sad shrug, Maria concluded, "As you see, we still have the Communists here."

We soon parted with hugs, happy to have met new friends. Later, Jeff and I made several trips to Hungary, bringing the widely requested children's Bible study materials.

Soviet tanks could indeed be seen throughout the city as we worked there during the '80s. An estimated 250,000 Soviet troops were stationed in Budapest. Some of their bunker hills were visible from the roads, and the army trucks and vehicles were much in evidence across the country.

Considered by many as the Paris of Eastern Europe, Budapest became one of our favorite spots behind the Iron Curtain. Occasionally, Jeff and I rented a bed and breakfast in a private home via the state tourist agency. That's how we first met Nora, a college student raised to be a Communist atheist. Like a rare orchid, innocent, exquisite and thirsty, she questioned our Christianity and dared to taste freedom.

When we told Nora of Christ and invited her to church, she was amazed to learn we believed God existed. She guided us through Budapest, lecturing on its history as we traipsed up the steps of Parliament, across famous bridges and lovely parks, on to Castle town, strolling through museums and cathedrals no longer in use. She spoke of communism, the party line and its absolute glory. We listened, quietly sharing how Christ had transformed our lives.

One evening Nora attended church with us and her life was changed, ours too from her precious friendship. We met intermittently through the years, until she left for the Soviet Union to study Russian literature. Nora fell in love with a premier Jewish violinist there. Their decision to marry was a blow to his career, as Soviets were not permitted to marry Hungarians. They were regarded as too Westernized.

We met at her mother's home shortly before her marriage. Jeff and I wanted to give the couple a honeymoon in Vienna as a wedding gift, but Nora disappeared into the Soviet's vastness, too fearful of reprisals to permit any contact between us.

Thus, even in Eastern Europe there were degrees. The farther from the West one traveled, the more difficult life became. The persecution in Hungary, Yugoslavia and Poland, though serious, was not as harsh as in countries like Romania, Bulgaria and the U.S.S.R. The difference was enormous and despite the degrees, the variances denoted loss of freedom.

8

God's Faithfulness

INSPIRED BY OUR VISIT with the Lazlos, Jeff and I left Budapest and traveled on Highway 5 east through Szeged, Hungary's third largest city. Miles of towering sunflower crops brightened the roadside, relieving the tedium of the snail-paced traffic. A steady stream of army trucks clogged the busy two-lane route.

We watched in fascination as tiny East German Trabants, initially, fabricated of pressed wood, and Russian Ladas edged into the lane of oncoming traffic to pass the heavy trucks. Soon Jeff was doing the same.

The nearer we came to Romania the more the landscape changed, in ways visible and invisible. The colors grew bleaker and the roads more horrid. We tried to avoid hitting the drunks who wandered along the highway, the Gypsies in horse-drawn covered wagons and others on bicycles.

In Szeged, we stopped again to ensure nothing incriminating remained in the cab and camper. Jeff and I planned to slip through customs as ordinary tourists. Mark had warned us if they discovered the Bibles, we would be charged with smuggling contraband, and the vehicle confiscated.

I felt exhilarated. Finally, we would see what life was like for those for whom we prayed so fervently. Still the border loomed. We knew from inside reports that each summer about twenty-five vehicles containing smuggled Bibles were confiscated at Romania's borders.

From Szeged we traveled through Kiszombor, Mako and Nadlac. The tension within escalated. I panicked near Pecica, about twenty minutes

31

before we reached the border. Strange, it never occurred to me I would be frightened. I stared at my trembling hands and knew I could not go forward.

An unfamiliar desperation churned like spoiled milk in my stomach. Shaken, I prayed for peace. Jeff failed to notice. His gaze was on the road, and perhaps he battled his own insecurities. Each kilometer brought us closer, and my panic grew. I glanced across at Jeff. "I'm scared. Will you pray with me?"

He gave me an understanding look that spoke volumes and stretched one hand to cover mine. "In the name of Jesus, Lord, we're asking You to remove Jeana's fear. Fill her with Your Holy Spirit right now to do the work You've called her to do."

I've never seen a truer example of the Scripture that says, whenever two or more of you pray concerning crisis or anything, I will be in the midst of you (Matt. 18:19, 20). God's peace filled me and as we proceeded, I was amazingly relaxed.

Soon we were processed through the Hungarian outpost, and we crossed the border into Romania. In a line about one-quarter mile long, scores of vehicles waited for customs. Guards toting rifles were posted along the route. Some of them stopped us to ask for food, pointing to their stomachs and mouths in a universal language. I passed out chocolate bars and bananas, receiving smiles and thanks from the young soldiers.

Jeff steered the camper past them into a special lane for Westerners, with only a few cars. The grimy border station held one covered port for East Europeans, and one for Westerners. There was a wooden bench alongside to unload luggage and belongings for inspection. The customs office was an aging yellowed stucco building. On the side of the structure, there was a ticket window where officials deposited passports for approval stamps. Visitors also purchased the required *lei* currency for the duration of their visas there.

A hardened police officer took our passports and a waiting game began. For hours, the customs officials and guards sought to intimidate us with their scrutiny, watching us from different angles, walking around our vehicle in silent speculation. Then finally, an officer ordered, "Get out. Open the back!"

Jeff opened the camper door and the official in charge studied us carefully at close range. "Do you have any guns, Bibles or pornography?" Communists feared these three items the most and seldom failed to ask this question.

I pointed to several maps, magazines and books we'd previously arranged about the camper in anticipation of his query. "There are our books."

They commanded us to empty everything onto the long wooden bench. Every suitcase was opened, each article of clothing examined. They entered the camper, knocked on walls, measured spaces, disassembled beds, tables and repeatedly pounded on cabinets, walls and floors in search of contraband. I stood outside and peered through the door, chatting with the supervisor about places to visit while Jeff tried to steer them from problem areas inside.

The customs officials who were measuring the vehicle's interior pointed right at two of the hidden compartments and one of them declared, "There's a secret compartment here and here."

God's calm never left me. I stood there fearless, overcome with the realization, we were carrying God's Word to His people, and He would ensure it reached them. The responsibility rested on His shoulders, not mine. We were merely the instruments He'd chosen. Silently though, my prayers flew heavenward: Father, this is Your Word, for Your people—have Your way. It's up to You.

The border supervisor glanced from me to the insistent customs official. Decisively, he shook his head, determining we didn't look or act like smugglers. He ordered the vehement guards from the RV. Praise the Lord for His mighty hand of deliverance. Throughout the next decade and beyond, God continued to miraculously open doors for us as He had that day.

Later, I learned, the guards were eager to tear up the vehicles because they received a promotion if contraband was discovered. But, if they tore up the vehicle and found nothing, their supervisor risked a demotion. Thus his hesitation when we didn't fit the smugglers' profile. Once they suspected a pair of purple candles we carried were rockets. Another time they were sure the milk powder in the camper was cocaine. Once they drilled into the walls of a courier vehicle between rows of Bibles, missing them entirely. God was ever faithful.

9

Confrontation in Arad

ON THAT FIRST COURIER TRIP, after our Romanian visas were approved, Jeff and I entered the country at the border town of Nadlac about midnight. We drove on about 150 kilometers to the city of Arad, where we planned to spend the night and rendezvous with Paul the next morning.

Smoldering clouds veiled the moon and stars. In the eerie dark, elderly stooped women wielding bundles of straw swept the grimy streets. We parked in front of a rundown hotel on the main thoroughfare and climbed out of the camper. The two of us walked to the entrance and Jeff opened the door for me to precede him. Inside, a hulking man blocked our path. He motioned for us to leave. Seven or eight of his cronies stood nearby watching.

"We'd like a room for the night," Jeff said.

The man pointed to the exit.

"There's no place else to go," I protested.

The hulk refused to move.

Jeff tried in vain to make him understand we merely wanted a room. Finally, we accepted defeat and left. "There must be another hotel." Jeff glanced about doubtfully as we reached the truck. Curiously, a stranger materialized, seemingly out of nowhere, and in reasonably good English offered to direct us to a nearby campground.

Jeff coasted behind the fellow's auto down a side road leading out of town. After about fifteen minutes of driving, I said, "This is spooky out here in the middle of nowhere with only trees and more trees and bushes. Anything could happen."

"He might be an angel guiding us. There's just one of him. What could happen?"

"Plenty," I said with a worried frown. "Who knows what we'll find. Maybe he's—" How could I put my fears of the unknown into words?

"Nonsense," Jeff interrupted as we glided into a wooded camping area with a small inn. Our escort seemed to vanish mysteriously into the night.

Jeff went inside to reserve us a spot. While I waited, a man with protruding eyes emerged from the surrounding woods. Frightened, I locked the vehicle. With a determined stride, he circled the truck and tried to open the doors. He kept circling, peering into the windows and fiddling with the door handles. What was keeping Jeff?

The man swore, kicking out at the fenders and tires. He pressed his face against the glass, staring at me. To my relief, I saw Jeff returning. At his approach, the man melted from sight.

Though we might never agree on whether the stranger who led us there was angel or fiend, we stayed, as we were to meet Paul in Arad the next morning.

10

Dressing the Part

AFTER A SHORT NIGHT'S REST, Jeff and I drove into Arad. The people milling about could have stepped out of a 1930s movie set of the poor side of town. Our arrangement was to meet Paul in front of the train station and follow him briefly until he signaled it was safe to approach. He melded into the crowd so well, we almost lost sight of him.

Despite our efforts to blend in, we stuck out as Westerners. Eventually, Jeff and I learned how important it was to wear nondescript clothing and shoes purchased in Eastern Europe. I also avoided jewelry and makeup. It merely drew unwanted attention. A person's demeanor was also telling. The art of slumped shoulders and walking without a spring in our steps took practice. We refrained from speaking whenever there was a possibility of being overheard. Our voices and accents were certain to give us away.

Through the years, Jeff and I became so adept at disguises that one of the better hotels in Bulgaria once refused to allow us to enter, believing we were natives. Only Westerners and those with money or special connections frequented these hotels. It's incredible how Jeff, at six-feet-four and with red hair, could have been mistaken for a Bulgarian. There's a certain weariness associated with the Communist-dominated third-world countries that grows on people like moss. After a decade of ministry in the East Bloc, it shrouded us like a heavy cloak we could no longer discard.

In elevators and public places in Romania, people often chatted to us in their own language. Somehow, we managed to respond without speaking. Similarly, in cities such as Moscow and Kiev, Soviets would spot my watch and, assuming I was a native, stop me on the streets, subways, trams or in the shops to ask the time. Instead of replying, I lifted my wrist in a preoccupied manner so they could see the dial.

On one trip to Leningrad, now St. Petersburg, Ruth, a vital member of the DOHI team that worked for ten years to produce Thomas Nelson's *Russian Open Bible Study Bible*, accompanied us as a translator. Her family, with thousands of other Pentecostals wanting to avoid Christian persecution, had escaped the Soviet Union, sneaking across the border into China where she was born. Mao Zedong's *Great Leap Forward* produced a horrible famine across China, one in which Ruth nearly died of starvation. As the famine spread, Mao ordered all non-nationals to leave or they would be shot. Hundreds of thousands became stateless refugees. Ruth's family was placed in Australia among a large Russian-speaking community and eventually settled in Canada. The Great Chinese Famine resulted in an estimated eighteen to forty-five million deaths, the largest in human history.

When Ruth and I visited the wife of Anatoly Vlasov in Moscow, the famous Christian Russian poet who had spent five years in prison for his faith, Ruth translated for me. Before we left, Anatoly's wife took me in her warm, pudgy arms. She gave me a bear hug and a Russian style kiss smack on the lips, exclaiming, "You are a true Russian."

We had flown Aeroflot from East Berlin into Leningrad. During much of the ten-day stay, I was quite ill with fever. The water at our hotel was red, so I bought 7 UP from the dollar shop to drink instead.

As was typical of these jaunts, the Soviets expected us to show up for meals and tourist activities. Under cover of night, we rode the subways and trams from one contact to the next and arrived back at our hotel in the early a.m. We slept two or three hours, and then it was off to breakfast. Our group split up to accomplish more.

Missionaries were often attacked spiritually. The stronger the Communist hold on the area, the greater the battle. Romanian Pastor Benjamin Cocar once shared a joke, confirming the locals were familiar with Satan's antics as well.

It went like this: Nixon traveled to Moscow to meet with Brezhnev, and was quite taken with a red phone on the Soviet president's desk. When he inquired about it, Brezhnev explained, it was a direct line to Satan. Brezhnev left his office briefly, and Nixon couldn't resist picking up the phone.

An operator said, "Hot line to Satan. Deposit twenty-five cents please."

Enticed by the idea, Nixon returned to the United States determined to have his own red phone. He persuaded Congress to appropriate the funds. At last, when it was installed, Nixon sat at his desk and picked up the receiver.

An operator came on the line and said, "Hot line to Satan. Deposit twenty-five dollars, please."

Nixon sputtered, "It was only twenty-five cents in Moscow."

"It's a local call there," the operator explained.

On that Soviet journey with Ruth and Jeff, I was under constant mental and spiritual attack. During the few hours available for sleep, I found myself on my knees praying for inner peace.

The situation worsened as we prepared to leave the country. Initially when we'd entered, much of the money to be distributed for aid was listed on my customs declaration. Worn down from illness and battling the enemy, I scrambled to pack.

At the airport, customs quickly processed Jeff and Ruth. But I was told, "*Nyet*! No! Go back." My thoughts raced. What if they demanded an explanation of where the cash and various items I had declared had gone? I prayed, feeling as if there were no strength left within me and worried I might burst into tears in front of everyone. In an effort to get permission to join them, I pointed across the divide to where Jeff and Ruth stood. Soldiers with rifles motioned me back, shouting, "*Nyet. Nyet.*"

"Please, I'm an American. He's my husband." As I watched Jeff and Ruth on the other side of the metal barriers being urged to depart, I struggled to compose myself.

Jeff tried to break away and cross the barrier to join me, but the militia halted him.

Dejected, I glanced away, praying for strength.

"Jeana," Jeff called softly.

I raised my gaze to his, warmed by the love and reassurance I saw there.

"Here." He tossed me a small package of Kleenex before moving past and vanishing from sight.

His kindness broke me, and tears trailed down my cheeks. I don't often cry, and when I do it's when I'd least like to. God, however, used my tears to soften one of the guards who approached customs on my behalf. He discovered they believed I was a defecting Soviet citizen.

The irony was that Ruth, the Russian among us, was simply accepted as a Westerner, while my disguise actually worked against me. Usually when ministering in Eastern Europe, I took the precaution of dressing like a Westerner at borders and airports and like the locals inside the country. Since I was ill, I had neglected to change back into Western clothes. Thankfully, I was eventually cleared to depart.

Later at home in Texas, my dear friend and mentor LaJewel Shrack, our Bible Study Fellowship lecturer, phoned. I told her how difficult the trip had been. "LaJewel, I felt as if I was under constant attack. I had to get up in the night and spend hours on my knees praying to get through it."

LaJewel, who for years had been one of my most faithful encouragers, reminded me, "It behooves us as Christians to expect to have to spend nights on our knees."

She was so right, I thought, immediately chastened. As Christians we accept God's grace and mercy yet are often caught unaware when adversity comes. Satan strikes and we've forgotten there is even a battle. In the New Testament, Christ admonishes us to be "wise as serpents and harmless as doves," (Matt. 10:16). The wise Christian kept her lamp filled and trimmed and was not caught in the darkness (Matt. 25:1–10).

11

Romania

DURING THAT FIRST TRIP into Eastern Europe in the summer of 1980, Jeff and I had met with Paul in Arad and cemented plans to rendezvous the next day in Bucharest, Romania's capital. We arrived there feeling sticky and grimy, longing for a bath and a place to wash clothes. The pickup camper did not include shower and bathroom facilities, despite giving the appearance of such amenities. Every spare inch of available space stored hidden Bibles.

Novices that we were, we parked downtown, checked into a hotel, bathed and then washed our clothes in the tub. Meanwhile, Maria, DOHI's European director, cruised into town and spotted the RV. Aghast, she ordered us to move it to the campground. "Keep yourselves and that RV out of sight!"

It became clear that any overt contact between DOHI couriers and the administrative staff placed the entire operation in jeopardy. Also, it was an absolute; the RVs with hidden Bibles were never to be compromised by association with any of the Christians we served.

The Communists made certain each church had an informer. Pastor Benjamin Cocar compared it to the familiar trash can. Just as everyone knew where the garbage was kept, congregations were forewarned and better off if they knew who was betraying them to the secret police. The greater danger was to be caught unaware. Informers may have even infiltrated the Christians with whom we worked.

Most churches had government appointed pastors. I've had a preacher shake my hand at the sanctuary door, then slip outside before he started the sermon to copy our license plate number. Ministers were routinely interrogated on Monday mornings and ordered to report on visitors. Those like Benjamin Cocar, who steadfastly refused to follow these guidelines, were threatened and persecuted.

Benjamin shared the story of a high-ranking Communist official who became a Christian and requested a secret baptism at home in his bathtub. Only the man, Benjamin and the church deacon were present. The next day the baptized official was called into his superior's office and fired. "The deacon reported the incident. There was no one else who could have," Benjamin said. "There were only the three of us, and I trusted that man with my life."

Jeff and I relied on the Holy Spirit for discernment. It was amazing how God directed us, revealing who could be trusted and whom to avoid. We never used our real names even when alone. Should the Christians we worked with in the East Bloc choose to report us, they only knew our pseudonyms, Phillip and Kathryn Jefferson. If the authorities checked at the borders, hotels, campgrounds or elsewhere, they wouldn't find anyone with those names. Officially, we were registered with our passports as Jeff and Jeana Kendrick.

DOHI's couriers drove the RVs filled with the smuggled Bibles behind the Iron Curtain. The Bibles were unloaded at the campgrounds and placed into dark heavy trash bags sealed with tape. These were then passed to a second team in a separate automobile who met with the persecuted believers and arranged for distribution of the literature and aid. Jeff often told our couriers if they were adept at grocery sacking, they were naturals for this job.

It might sound simple, but the process was a heart-thumping, adrenaline rush. Consider how armed militia routinely strolled through the campground while making rounds, not with guns in holsters, but with rifles ready to fire. The state owned and guarded these places.

The compartments had to be dismantled, and the RVs actually rocked some in the process. Couriers were most vulnerable with God's Word spread out everywhere and the cabinets, ceilings, walls and floors torn apart.

On one occasion, I slipped from the camper to ensure all was well, checking with team members stationed nearby to warn us when the militia approached. I decided to visit the camp's public ladies' room while out.

A woman from Holland approached me. "I don't know if you're doing what we think you're doing. Still I thought you should know, we can see through your shades when the light's on."

I hadn't realized how exposed we were while unpacking the Bibles. The mission was on a tight budget, yet we bought new shades ASAP when we arrived back in the West.

I sometimes theorized that most of the Westerners we came across in these places were probably Bible smugglers too. Anyone visiting those campgrounds might draw the same conclusion. Some of the facilities and conditions could be described as hair-raising.

Once I was accosted in the shower by three women who stole my soap. Naked, I held them off with water spray, yelling for Jeff at the top of my lungs. I was afraid they would steal my clothes and leave me stranded in the nude. There were no shower doors and my clothes hung on a nail between us.

The women, better dressed than most, mocked me in English, crudely ridiculing my plump body. Fortunately, Jeff heard me, and the ladies dispersed when he arrived.

Romanian friends, whom I later spoke with about the incident, thought the three might have been engaged by the secret police as a warning to me. When the incident occurred, Jeff and I were seasoned couriers. Reports had reached us that some of our teams had been questioned at the borders by authorities searching for Phillip and Kathryn Jefferson. From then on, Jeff waited for me outside the ladies' rooms at the various sites.

The mission RVs were often viewed as tourist attractions in Eastern Europe. This was problematic when striving to maintain a low profile. I recall one day in Sibu, when without any invitation on our part the native campers formed a line at our motor home door to tour the vehicle. By late afternoon, we were growing anxious. The time of our rendezvous was swiftly approaching, and the literature needed to be unloaded. Yet it was impossible to act amid the interested crowd's attention. Providentially, God blessed us with a summer rain. This sent the natives scattering to their tents, and we were able to begin the night's work. I never tired of the thrill of seeing God's handiwork.

After we emptied the secret compartments, everything had to be brought outside and put in the car. To carry one to five thousand books (the number varied with the RV size), packaged into one-by-three-foot rectangles, can be rather conspicuous. Consequently, we developed a clothesline strategy, draping wet garments or airing blankets across a rope anchored between two trees to form some sort of camouflage.

I'll never forget when the RV, the mission referred to as the Diamond, broke down on a major Romanian highway in stark daylight. Jeff ordered me to drive the Toyota station wagon alongside it. I was most reluctant but did so because there was no other option. The men swiftly unloaded the compartments and packed the entire station wagon with sacks of Bibles high enough to be seen through the windows. They threw blankets across the top and told me to take off. They stayed behind to repair the mechanical problems without fear of being caught.

There were guard posts scattered throughout the country where the militia halted traffic, spot-checking people and vehicles. To have the car packed with contraband on a busy highway was unnerving but being stopped at the various guard posts was worse, knowing a thin blanket was all that stood between discovery and me.

I prayed, and God faithfully allowed me to pass through without any problems. When stopped, I offered the militia chocolate bars to take home to their children. I felt more than ever like a housewife from Texas who was out of her depth. Since by then we were co-directors and equipped with so many wonderful people working with us, I took my inadequacies to our Lord, who provided strength, wisdom and grace.

12

High Stakes

EVENTUALLY, THE DAY CAME when our presence put the mission's RVs at risk. Jeff and I were becoming too well known. As co-directors of DOHI's literature distribution into Eastern Europe, we coordinated its courier program and deliveries behind the Iron Curtain.

Our caravan rolled into Sofia one fall, a season when tourists were fewer and more conspicuous. Midsummer delays had left us behind in our Bible deliveries, and it was already late October. Jeff and I drove the Citroën. Jill and Conrad Nolan from Texas and their kids were in the Diamond; Mike and Ellen from Florida in the fifth wheel; and John and Charlene and their children from California in the pickup camper. These couples were some of our most dedicated volunteers who returned annually to serve. Like most of the teams who came, they had jobs to resume in the States.

Once we arrived at our destination, a nearby hillside campground on the outskirts of Sofia, everyone, except the Nolans and us, left to catch flights back to the United States. Their vehicles were unloaded, and the Bibles were packed into the fifth wheel. John and Charlene took off in the pickup camper while Mike and Ellen left in our Citroën.

Jeff drove the fifth wheel. It could hold either 1,200 large Study Bibles or five thousand New Testaments. I rented a Lada for rendezvous—a chilling scenario, because it would be easy to trace the rental to our site. There we were with all those hidden Bibles, plus the sacked ones under the table and on the beds from the RVs we'd emptied.

Our first contact was a pastor who was under house arrest and in dire straits. The secret police had broken his mother's hand as a warning to him not to hold services. A code had been prearranged to alert him of our arrival. I phoned, speaking with a German accent, pretending it was a certain hotel, and was told I had the wrong number. This was the signal for one of his church members to meet us at the diner. We waited most of the afternoon in vain and decided to chance visiting him later.

Our nerves on edge, Jeff and I climbed into the Lada that evening and drove to the pastor's neighborhood. Just as we reached the roundabout where three streets converged and Jeff started to turn onto the pastor's street, the militia cornered us. Several of their autos zoomed in so close we couldn't move. Terrified, the two of us sat frozen, praying, expecting any second to be arrested.

What would they do to the pastor and his family if we were caught? Then in my mind, I saw the mission's RVs parked on the hillside. If we lost them, how could DOHI continue to deliver Bibles? Were Jill and Conrad and their children safe in the Diamond?

Then the militia eased the noses of their cars back, inches, enough to let us squeeze past. The Lada shot out into the night, Jeff driving as fast as he dared for the next hour and a half, the militia on our tails much of the time.

Finally, with a shudder, I realized we'd either lost them or they'd circled to the camp to find us. My brain raced as I tried to predict their next moves. We'd used our passports to rent the Lada and book our site. The militia could run the license plate numbers to identify us, and our location. Maybe they already had. The pounding in my chest slowed when we returned to the camp and all seemed well.

The next morning, I parked the Lada in front of the camp office. Jeff was in the fifth wheel behind me, and the Nolans trailed him in the Diamond. We all climbed out of our vehicles and joined the line of people waiting to get their passports returned. We planned to travel to a safer area.

As we stood in line, two black secret police sedans pulled up, a few men in suits got out and strode through the back door of the office. I watched through the front window as one of them spoke sharply to the clerk, who then moved aside, giving the men access to everyone's passports. The men flipped through them, then pocketed two small navy blue ones that looked American and started down the path.

My stomach heaved in protest at how vulnerable we were with the two RVs parked there, sacks of Bibles on the floor. To fully understand, one would need to know how we prayed and worked, and dreamed and schemed, day after day and year after year, developing methods to bring more of God's Word to these precious Christians who risked their lives again and again. Their only plea, "Please, can you give us Bibles?"

Jeff had designed and built the fifth wheel in our backyard in Texas. Initially, most of the other RVs' compartments only held about five hundred books. Jeff rebuilt them to hold many more. During our off months, DOHI's European offices often scheduled church meetings for us to speak at on behalf of persecuted believers and to highlight the courier ministry. One fall, after I had spoken to a Belgium congregation, a member donated $25,000 for the mission to buy a new courier RV.

Slowly, we saw God's mighty hand opening more doors. As the operation grew, we trained gifted individuals from all walks of life who gave up their vacations each year to smuggle the Word of God into Eastern Europe. And they paid for the fuel, one of our biggest expenses. They were carpenters, bankers, doctors, nurses, housewives and more.

The main emphasis at DOHI board meetings was on translation and printing, with minor funding assigned to courier operations. God was changing this too. So, as Jeff and I stood on that hill, praying the secret police weren't coming for us, we weren't looking at the loss of two RVs— but the loss of a lifeline to bring Bibles and help to persecuted Christians. Also, we feared they would suffer repercussions. The smallest clue might lead the authorities to them.

We waited on tenterhooks for about an hour and a half, before a visiting

Polish family was taken into custody. The rest of us breathed sighs of relief and were soon handed our passports.

Immediately, our group set out for the campground in Kazanlak and settled there. In the evening, we unloaded the Diamond, placing more sacks in the fifth wheel. The Nolans left in the Diamond the next morning for Austria, then on to Munich, Germany, to catch their flight to the US.

For five consecutive nights, Jeff and I drove great distances in the Lada to ensure there would be no traces leading to the fifth wheel, while disbursing the Bibles to the various pastors. For each night's run, we transferred the literature from the RV to the car in broad daylight, alongside the highway on the outskirts of town. At this stage, the campsite seemed too risky.

Later, word trickled back that the secret police had raided one of the churches, confiscating two bags of the Bibles. The rest were safely delivered, and our main contacts were never compromised. The Lord brought us victoriously through many such incidents. Jeff and I were in awe of God's grace and presence in our lives. What a joy to toil in His ministry.

13

Bulgaria

THAT FIRST SUMMER IN 1980, when Jeff and I naively parked in downtown Bucharest, Romania, at Maria's command we drove on to the campground. In the ensuing years, the two of us grew quite familiar with the ins and outs of such places. For example, the shower faucets refused to work for the casual visitor and no effort on our part sufficed to alter this. A small gift to the chief caretaker, though, accomplished wonders. He would turn on every sink and shower faucet, do a little mumbo-jumbo with the pipes, and presto there was water. A similar token ensured the gates, usually locked at 10:00 p.m., were opened as needed for our nightly rendezvous.

The highlight of every trip was meeting Christians. In true cloak and dagger style, we met Paul downtown on our debut jaunt to Bucharest and followed him on foot into an old-time photography shop. Caraman, slender and white-haired, greeted us with a twinkle in his eyes. He gestured toward the walls, indicating they were probably bugged, and turned the radio dial until music camouflaged the sound of our voices.

As Paul introduced us, Caraman asked with a look of concern, "Are those their real names?"

"I know better than that," Paul said.

"Good." Caraman gave a relieved nod.

Fascinated, we listened as they discussed the status and needs of the churches in Romania and various ongoing projects, which the mission financed. There was again that feeling of being a part of an endeavor, bigger and beyond ourselves. An onslaught of humility rushed through me and with it a compelling hunger to do everything I could to help these people.

After the Romanian Bibles we smuggled in were delivered, Jeff and I drove on to Bulgaria, while Paul flew to its capital, Sofia, to meet us. As novices, we weren't entrusted with the addresses of Christian contacts. The plan was to wait for Paul at a certain train station for the first ten minutes of every other hour until we connected. For two days, we arrived periodically as arranged, but there was no sign of Paul. The camper, parked a few blocks away, had Bulgarian Bibles hidden in the compartments. There was a sick churning in my stomach as I recognized the secret police with their black umbrellas, observing the entrance each time we arrived.

If a problem occurred, we were to phone the base in Austria, then speak in a prearranged code, and instructions would be forthcoming. Tension mounted as we called the base on the second night. The courier who answered was a novice and skittish about relaying any details in case the wires were tapped. Thus, he mangled the instructions. Unaware of this, Jeff and I continued with the initial schedule and left for Stara Zagora, a much smaller city, and began the every-two-hour train station routine again.

The two of us seemed to be the only foreigners in town. At the end of the second day, the police arrested Jeff, leaving me in the pickup while they took him off to jail. I prayed, fearing what would happen to us if they found the Bibles. I wasn't seasoned enough yet to worry about the camper or perceive its importance.

Bulgaria was nothing like Romania. Many of the Bulgarian Christians the mission worked with had been in exile or prison and they were slowly being released. Most of them returned to their homes as fervent as ever in their faith. The majority remained deeply underground in the aftermath of much persecution.

The struggle to obtain a city map in Bulgaria was fraught with peril. The government tourist bureau treated maps like state secrets. To get one, we risked drawing unwanted attention that could result in our being tailed by the secret police. People commonly followed and reported on friends to the local authorities. Fear was the prevailing sentiment. Yet God in His mercy continually gave us strength to overcome and filled our hearts with his peace and joy.

Romanian border searches were arduous, though within the country, security varied between provinces. Because of this lack of communication, overall surveillance was looser. By contrast, Bulgarian border searches were not quite as hair-raising, however, control within was more stringent. In the U.S.S.R., both border and inner controls were so steely as to be almost impenetrable. Still, with God, the impossible became possible.

When Jeff and I traveled, the feeling of oppression increased the farther into the East Bloc we went. When we journeyed from Vienna to Budapest, the difference was stark and oppressive, in Romania it became frightening, in Bulgaria smothering and in the Soviet Union one felt communism's strangling grip. After spending a few weeks in the U.S.S.R., one could almost hear the bells of freedom ringing in Romania.

As to the other nations of Eastern Europe, Poland was generally lax, so much so that DOHI set up a system of delivering Russian New Testaments there. Polish Christians could mail the NTs to the Soviet Union without the same concern of detection as would be experienced elsewhere. There were invariably risks in such ventures. Czechoslovakia was more difficult. Places like Iran and Albania were deadly, yet I knew couriers who made routine runs there.

Perhaps the average tourist never sensed this oppression to the degree missionaries did but attacking Satan on his home ground was cause for provocation. However, we had an assurance that Christ within us was stronger than our enemy, and through Him we could overcome all.

So, in Stara Zagora as I waited in the pickup for Jeff, who was in the police station down the block, I begged Christ to intercede on our behalf and He did. Of course, there were many prayers besides mine: Jeff's, the

Bulgarian Christians who were expecting the Bibles, our fellow couriers, the mission staff, our family and friends at home.

When the police couldn't locate an English translator for the interrogation, they were forced to release Jeff. I have since traveled to Stara Zagora on many occasions and generally found someone who spoke English or German with whom we could converse, especially in the hotels.

The original plan had been to deliver the Bibles remaining in the camper, then drive to DOHI's base in Thessaloniki, Greece, and reload. The mission had set up its Austrian and Greece bases with this in mind. The authorities could reasonably assume the couriers were merely tourists following a return route from their travels, and in this manner, the mission doubled the number of Bibles delivered.

Unsure of what else to do, Jeff and I smuggled the Scriptures back out of the country into Greece where we hoped to meet up with our team. Hot and tired, we arrived there in 114-degree weather. The pickup overheated and Jeff poured water in the radiator. We finally reached the base in Thessaloniki to find Paul and the rest of the DOHI team already there. Paul said the Bulgarian authorities had blackballed him, refusing to let him off the plane in Sofia, thereby forcing him to fly on to Athens. He immediately phoned the Austrian base, arranging for Mark to travel to Bulgaria with the addresses of those to whom we were to deliver the Bibles.

Mark had been waiting for us in another city. The novice courier who fielded our call intentionally gave us the wrong information, fearing someone else had learned our code. He somehow thought we would realize this. Naturally, everyone was disappointed. Paul bemoaned the fact we had actually smuggled Bibles out of Bulgaria. "You should have buried them," he said. "You could have retrieved them later."

Jeff shook his head. "There was no way to get a shovel. We tried. It's impossible to buy such simple items. Besides there weren't any roads wandering off into nowhere. Everything's too tightly controlled."

Paul insisted, "You should have found a way." He clasped his hand to his forehead and said gently, "Ma-ma-mia! Christians are begging for Bibles there, and you two smuggle them out of the country."

Jeff and I regrouped, did laundry and enjoyed a swim in the Mediterranean. We then reloaded the compartments, which had been emptied in Romania and Hungary, and headed back to Bulgaria with a full load. I had learned a valuable lesson that stayed with me. I later passed it on to those I helped train. Never let anyone send you out in the field without alternative plans, preferably A, B and C. Make sure all backups are viable. Don't hesitate to ask questions. And never rendezvous at obvious places like train stations where you'll surely be observed if there's a setback.

The joy on the faces of the pastors and Christians to whom we gave the Bibles, made every difficult moment worthwhile. Relationships forged on that trip continue to be an important part of our lives. This week I received word Brother Caraman died. Until the end, he served God, church and country faithfully, doing more behind the scenes than most will ever know.

14

No Turning Back

WHEN WE ARRIVED BACK at the Austrian base after our first trip into Eastern Europe, it seemed as if months, instead of weeks, had passed. Soon our period abroad would end.

Shortly before we left for the States, Paul Popov took us aside. "I'd like you both to seriously contemplate returning for a full year next spring. God has given you a natural gift for this work."

Amazingly, our hearts and minds concurred. Jeff and I committed to serve a full year, and our lives were changed irrevocably. Thirty-seven years later, I still work with DOHI. Those years in Eastern Europe were blessed.

Yet as our ministry commitment increased, the heat from Satan rose accordingly. Remember, in the Garden of Eden how Satan initially approached Eve, though Adam certainly had his turn later? Back at home in Texas, I felt trapped in this intense mental warfare. It would last days and then reignite just when I seemed to have conquered it.

Scripture bears this out: "For we wrestle not against flesh and blood, but against principalities, against powers, against the rulers of the darkness of this world, against spiritual wickedness in high places," (Eph. 6:12).

We get through difficult seasons by yielding to God's strength. "For the weapons of our warfare are not carnal, but mighty through God to the pulling down of strong holds; Casting down imaginations and every high thing which exalteth itself against the knowledge of God, and bringing into captivity every thought to the obedience of Christ;" (2 Cor. 10:4, 5).

Events climaxed the following spring, six weeks before our trip to

Europe. I can't think of a morning when I felt closer to God. I was in the middle of doing my Bible Study Fellowship lesson when a long-distance call came for Mark Richards, a missionary friend, who was visiting us on his journey south to Belize. Mark's story of how he founded an organization that provides thousands of wheelchairs to the needy around the world is fascinating.

Yet on that day, my Bible and lesson in hand, I called Mark to the phone. He and Jeff had a come-along tied to a tree in order to move a trailer. Mark went inside and I stayed behind for a few minutes to help. I was reading my lesson and thinking what a gorgeous day it was and how great our Lord is.

I don't remember the tree falling, or Jeff's shout of warning as it struck the back of my head and then my shoulders as I crumpled, unconscious, to the ground. Still God's protection was ever present. A stump sticking up, stopped the tree from pinning me to the ground.

As if from a distance, I awoke to hear Jeff shouting for Mark. Then I was lying on a board in the foyer, choking, unable to move. I asked Jeff to call LaJewel Shrack, the leader of my Bible Study Fellowship class, and ask her to pray. From our study group of about 450 members a prayer chain began. Jeff then phoned for an ambulance, and Dr. Crocket met us at the hospital.

Jeff's parents and our friends Bill and Diane Burnich came as well. Dr. Crocket diagnosed a complex fracture of the seventh and eighth vertebrae and told me I was fortunate. If it had been my sixth vertebra, I would have been paralyzed instantly.

I spent the week in the hospital, unable to move. The nurses rolled me from one side to the other periodically. Because the nerves from the injured vertebrae affected my stomach, I was constantly nauseated.

At Jeff's request, the doctor released me on the condition that, initially, I would have continual care and remain confined to bed. Jeff's mother took splendid care of me, as did Jeff. He made marvelous orange juice and eggs. Though I improved, our family and friends were concerned because we still wanted to serve as missionaries overseas that spring.

I wondered, Lord, is this what You want me to do? Often those we hoped to serve had no one to turn to but God as they suffered poverty, persecution and oppression. God was urging me to trust Him as well, and I yielded willingly, leaving for Europe as planned.

15

Georgi and Florica

FOR OUR SECOND YEAR serving overseas, Jeff and I flew KLM. The airline offered missionaries a 15 percent discount. We shipped my VW Golf to Rotterdam and, thinking we had become quite savvy, booked lodging ahead in Amsterdam at a bed and breakfast recommended in *LET'S GO EUROPE*.

What a mass of luggage we had! Jeff toted my sewing machine and his ham radio, plus two carry-ons. I was unable to help due to the tree accident. Our checked baggage included an oversized trunk and three suitcases packed with peanut butter, popcorn, corn starch, fitted king sheets, regular-size bath towels and various other items unavailable in Austria.

When we arrived at Holland's megalopolis by the North Sea, with its tangled web of canals, we were charmed. White-gabled, dark-brick homes and storefronts whizzed past, the taxi's meter ticking up to about fifty dollars (and it was an extremely good year for the dollar). The cab stopped at the narrow three-story guest house where we were booked.

Jeff made three or four excursions, huffing up the formidable front steps, to pile the gear into the lobby. After we registered, the tall, dignified proprietress led us up a tight-winding staircase to the third floor. We knew then, we'd made a mistake.

I chuckled as Jeff jaunted up and down the stairs, hauling all our baggage. Finally finished, he collapsed on the bed, exhausted and jetlagged.

The next morning we feasted on Dutch coffee, cream, eggs, butter and rolls. Mmm . . . they were superb. After breakfast, we caught the train to Rotterdam, collected my VW Golf from the ship and drove on to Austria.

Still through the years, Jeff and I came to view Amsterdam as a place of respite. Periodically, we would ship cars and RVs from the US and then pick them up at the Rotterdam port.

———————————

IN PART, OUR FIRST YEAR in Europe as full-term missionaries remains a blur, the trips we made obscured by the hundreds of journeys that followed. Yet certain highlights prevail, never to be forgotten, such as secret meetings with Christians like Georgi and his wife Florica who risked a great deal for the cause of Christ.

Georgi's smile spread across his face, scratching indelible lines at the corners of his mouth and eyes, a smile reflected in his amber gaze and the pudgy cheeks set in his angular face. Lank sandy hair fell around the bald spot on his head. Tall and stocky, he had large hands that had suffered electrical shocks in torture sessions during Communist interrogations.

We were all in our early thirties, though Florica's lined, worn face and sad opaque eyes made her look older. Tall, thin and stooped, with coarse, tired gray hair, her demeanor was fervent and earnest.

They had three young children and a small flat in the middle of thousands of others in the concrete gray crumbling world of apartments, which thus advertised communism's economic and social failure, as well as its intrusive determination to control and manipulate those unfortunate enough to be caught in its painful grip.

It generally fell to me to initiate contact, navigating alone on foot, after Jeff dropped me off in the midst of blocks and blocks and miles and miles of flats where each one looked like its neighbor. My journeys through these mazes of Communist gray were one of life's ironies as I had an awful sense of direction.

Like David, God directed my path. "He maketh my feet like hinds' feet: and setteth me upon my high places. He teacheth my hands to war;

so that a bow of steel is broken by mine arms. . . . Thou hast enlarged my steps under me; so that my feet did not slip," (Psalms 18:34, 35, 37).

Time and time again, when I went out to set up a rendezvous, to verify certain contacts were in town, to deliver desperately needed funds or a manuscript which required proofing, God led me safely to each destination.

As I drew near Florica and Georgi's flat, my racing heart nearly exploded, fearful lest a neighbor or dog or watching member of the dreaded *securitate* should notice me. From the street, I slipped into their courtyard, longing to be invisible. The buildings formed a huge rectangle around a courtyard of dirt with a few clumps of dead grass or weeds.

The grimy glass doors of each unit had buzzers and an intercom for those without keys in order to request entry. Inside on the ground floor were mailboxes, apartments, a small elevator and concrete steps leading up, perhaps fifteen floors.

Consider how this simple procedure of visiting a friend was fraught with danger of exposure. In the courtyard, there might be residents, friends and neighbors coming and going. Any one of them could expose me with a word, a phone call or a shout. A curious child might notice the difference in my shoes, dress, hair or walk.

Florica and Georgi might be under surveillance. What if the main door was closed, which meant locked, instead of ajar, and someone leaned over my shoulder just as I spoke into the intercom, hearing Georgi's voice clearly answering my veiled request?

A brand-new set of impediments faced me when I stepped inside, still visible through the glass door to passersby. What if I didn't know our contact's apartment number? Suppose someone curious wandered in to investigate while I struggled to decipher from the names on mailboxes which flat to call on?

Suppose someone asked me a question? One spoken word would identify me as a foreigner. What if DOHI's contact lived on the ground floor and, as sometimes happened, a group of children or older men or women sat on the front stoop, watching to see who I would visit? Any mistake on my part could have brought about Georgi and Florica's immediate arrest, leaving their children to the care of family or neighbors, if they were fortunate.

There were still the steps or elevator to negotiate and finally the knock on the door, waiting, hoping no stranger would approach. Swiftly, Florica would draw me in, kiss both my cheeks, exclaiming, "*Pace, Pace*," the Romanian Christian greeting of peace. Her face lit with urgency, she would fold her hands as if in prayer, meaning they had been praying for us to come soon.

Then she'd draw me into the living room where we knelt, praising God for His blessings. Afterward, Georgi would ask in Romanian about Jeff, then pantomime with the Bible in his hand, "Did you bring Bibles?"

At my nod, they beamed with excitement and joy. Often Jeff joined us then, knowing when I failed to return at the prearranged time that he was to come up. Then Florica would disappear into the kitchen to cook while Georgi called one of his German-speaking friends to translate. Soon a feast, by Romanian standards, was set before us. Florica avidly watched our every bite, happy to have given their best. Wherever we traveled, this was the case. One family we knew saved the meat they received in a package from abroad each year to serve us.

On one visit to Florica and Georgi, while we were eating, they spoke eagerly, unable to restrain their enthusiasm. As we ate, the translator explained, "Such a meal we're eating, I've never had before in my life. Only Communist officials in my country are permitted to eat such. It is forbidden for others to do so." His eyes big, he pointed to his plate. "Tonight we have meat. And what a meat, rabbit, struck down on the highway and no one saw. So my friend," he gestured proudly to Georgi, "acquired this special treat to serve you."

I felt ill, though I tried to smile at each reluctant bite. We always endeavored to eat whatever was set before us, not wanting to offend these dear ones who had so little.

The interpreter ate gustily. "There is no meat to be had in Romania."

We gathered he was a young Christian, and a bundle of nerves. That night when we rendezvoused for the Bible drop off, he accompanied Jeff and me in order to lead us to where we'd meet Georgi.

Jeff stopped the Diamond RV alongside the route and, after Georgi arrived, followed him down a winding bumpy road. While we were transferring the Bibles, a couple of cars pulled up and we dove back into the Diamond. Jeff drove down the road, the rest of us holding on, stumbling around the Hefty Garbage Bags filled with Bibles strewn across the floor.

The frightened young man, almost squealing in his agitation about what would happen if he were caught, amused me. As serious as the situation was, I had a hard time concealing my laughter. I never expected to see a persecuted Christian as scared as I was.

Despite the comedy of errors, the trip was successful. But we never again permitted those we served to see or know in what vehicle we traveled or how we brought the Bibles. After that, the mission provided rental cars or an extra car from the Austrian base for transfers.

Suppose the young man had turned informer and tipped off the border guards. On subsequent trips we could have been followed and our Christian contacts arrested. These things happened. One young missionary back home in America sent a newsletter to eleven close friends in the US. Somehow, it landed in the hands of Romanian authorities, resulting in many arrests.

———————————

THE ORADEA CAMPGROUND WAS one we had visited often. On a previous trip, Jeff and I had scheduled a Bible drop with Georgi for 7:00 p.m. We arrived at the camping place with little time left to maneuver, which meant we needed to rush to get the compartments taken apart, unloaded and put back together. The Bibles also had to be sacked and secretly removed from the RV to the car. And finally, the drive into the country for the night's rendezvous must be undertaken.

Once again the problem lay in the curiosity of the neighboring Romanian campers, who kept knocking at the camper door, wanting to see inside. As this went on for several hours, Jeff and I grew concerned.

It was one of those gorgeous sunny days, not a cloud in the sky. Large green oaks shaded tourists from heat. Some milled around the concession stand buying snacks. Aside from us, the greatest attraction was a comparatively small shallow pool with green-brackish water and floating brown debris. Still, it was equipped with a primitive wave machine that left the children in low-tech heaven.

Throughout the grounds, tents were crowded one next to the other, some even in trees, and we were parked between the lot with no privacy. Stomach churning, I wondered how we were going to manage. Jeff and I exchanged troubled glances over the heads of our guests and never stopped praying.

Abruptly, thunder rumbled across the clear skies, black clouds rolled in and a torment of rain poured down, sending everyone running for their tents. Alone at last, we praised God for His marvelous intervention and set to work with the sense we'd just witnessed a miracle.

When the Bibles were sacked and the compartments together again the rain slowed to a drizzle that allowed us to move the bags quickly into the car without detection. Later, at the drop, the night skies were clear, the crescent of a moon lighting the dark road where we made the exchange.

Through the years, we made many trips. On yet another journey as we rolled into the same campground, Jeff and I were rather unnerved when the militia insisted that we park next to the concession. Throughout the day, an American rendition of the song, "He's Got the Whole World in His Hands" blared through the loudspeakers across the grounds. We didn't know what to think. Were they on to us? Was this a coincidence? A way of showing favor to the Americans? Needless to say, we were extraordinarily cautious. Thankfully, we concluded the song playing was merely a show of favor among the populace. God surprised us continually with his marvelous care and encouragement for us in His ministry.

16

Veselin and Magda

DURING THE '70s in a countrywide crackdown in Bulgaria, the Communists arrested many of the pastors working with Door of Hope International. Sadly, another minister had reported them. Those he betrayed were imprisoned or sent into exile.

As Jeff and I came on the scene in the '80s, many of these same pastors were being released. Our job was to establish contact, offer assistance and set up new distribution lines for Bibles.

Grace, an American and second-generation Bulgarian, translated for us. Her petite, matronly appearance blended well with the natives. She also helped manage the base in nearby Thessaloniki.

From DOHI Sweden, stacks of files detailing the mission's contacts and activities of the last two decades were dispersed to us for study. It was a trust that was not taken lightly. With this background information in mind, we searched out connections, who in some cases, had died or, in the interest of survival, had moved or gone deeply underground.

Early on, we met with Pastor Veselin and his wife Magda, a microbiologist. His father had suffered in the previous purge and as a result, they were extremely cautious.

The natural temptation would have been for them to accept our dollars, or at least, trade us the Bulgarian currency, *leva*, we needed for dollars. Though illegal, it was commonly done. Dollars bought things *leva* never could, like access to a doctor for a sick child, meat or a desperately needed car part. Still they were steadfast in their refusal to accept any personal gain.

The couple soon became the nucleus of our distribution line across Bulgaria. They always welcomed us joyfully to their home, and Magda and her mother fed us delightful meals. Through the years we became close friends. One cannot remember Veselin without recalling his wide smile, gentle demeanor and true Christ-like humility. Magda worked with him in the ministry. The two went on to establish more than one hundred churches, bringing Gypsies, Turks and their own people to know the Lord. They were an inspiration to us throughout our ministry as were so many of the Christians we served.

17

Friends at Home and Abroad

ONE OF OUR MOST DIFFICULT contacts to locate was Stefan. Jeff and I searched for him in earnest, compiling maps of various cities, which was not an easy task. When we attempted to buy these *state documents* from hotels, bookstores and train stations, we were often questioned sharply and tailed in the aftermath.

One time I tried to convince a hotel clerk in Stara Zagora to give us a map. She pointed to the Communist Blue Book, which she adhered to strictly for methodical instructions on every situation, and refused. "Americans are dangerous terrorists. Your evening news is proof of the lawless killings and terror in your country." State workers were so indoctrinated, it was impossible to convince her otherwise. Fear prevailed.

Once, during a Bulgarian jam convention, visiting Soviet officials asked for the Bulgarian's recipe. The Bulgarians exclaimed, "Comrades, we follow the Kremlin's Five Year Plan for making jam exactly."

Flagrant persecution and arrests had frightened most citizens into docile obedience. Informers were everywhere. One pastor begged us to bring copies of *Fox's Book of Martyrs*. "We are cowards in need of revival," he said. "It is not easy to be a Christian here and risk becoming a martyr."

Ultimately, Jeff and I obtained a map of Shumen and visited the addresses in Stefan's file. Often, former connections had moved two or three times since the mission had last contacted them. In our quest to find Stefan and others, we crept into apartment buildings, studied the mailboxes for clues, then stole quietly upstairs, frequently hitting yet another dead end. We saw an abundance of black wreaths on the doors for the deceased.

Eventually, we found Stefan and his family in town, residing in a small stucco house with a yard. His sixteen-year-old son, Nicky, who spoke English, translated as Stefan confided with a strained look, "I have recently returned home after six years in exile. Authorities deported me to a distant village near the Romanian border where I was forced to work as a brick layer. Any contact with my family was forbidden."

He led us downstairs to a basement he'd built for worship services. "I allowed the children to attend services, including my own two boys. For this crime, I was banished. It is illegal for minors to go to church even if their parents want them to."

We trooped back upstairs and talked for hours about the persecution challenging Christians and God's preserving grace. Stefan placed a hand on his eldest son's shoulder. "Nicky was eleven when I was arrested and sent into exile. Still, he learned to love Jesus. He chose to be baptized, and he witnessed to his friends while I was away. Now that I am home, the sanctuary is again filled with young and old who know of the Lord's goodness and love."

I admired his courage and dedication yet had to ask, "Won't the authorities arrest you for permitting the young people to attend?"

"We are all in God's hands," he said. He showed us a secret path out of the house that had protected them so far. "What would you have me do? Bar the sanctuary doors against the young? Forbid them the right to worship in church? Impossible to deny my Lord to one of these little ones."

Stefan, Diana and their two young boys were an attractive family, with their dark hair and eyes and fair complexions. The light of Bulgaria rested within them, willing to be spent for the love of Christ. When asked if they would accept Bible shipments to distribute, they never hesitated. They remained an integral part of the network we established until Stefan died under mysterious circumstances in 1989. Jeff and I were shocked, and we mourned Stefan, all the while praying for his family's safety and comfort.

LIKE STEFAN, STOYIAN BUKOV WAS difficult to find. He was a pastor of religious and philosophical eminence who had recently returned from exile. One evening, with Grace to translate, Jeff and I set out to visit Stoyian. We wore nondescript trench coats and rode the bus to attract less attention.

The three of us got off several stops before his place, unhappy when a swarm of fellow passengers debarked as well. We strolled off toward a less congested area, gradually isolating ourselves from the crowd.

Then Grace unwittingly spoke a word or two of English aloud. She stopped speaking immediately, horror-stricken by her lapse. A woman in the departing crowd glanced back sharply and turned to follow us.

In desperation, Grace began a monologue with us in Bulgarian as a cover up. The woman in pursuit remained undeterred. She moved closer each time we entered buildings to check the mailboxes, as if wanting to discover what we were up to.

This went on for a while, though we tried to lose her. Finally, in exasperation, Jeff whirled, whipped out his camera and flashed the woman's picture. She fled. We now had an incriminating picture of her in a place where she didn't belong.

The buildings we'd visited were merely decoys to throw her off the trail. The rest of our evening was spent in similar attempts to confuse anyone who might be shadowing us.

Friends there shared a standard joke that made the rounds. Two Bulgarians had stayed out late one night; the next morning the one who slept in was arrested. The inference was everyone reported on their neighbors and local justice could be as simple as who awakened earliest to inform first.

Several evenings later, Magda's mother led us to Stoyian's apartment. We enjoyed a wonderful interview and he requested the mission's help to leave the country. As we left his home, we heard shouts and saw the militia racing upstairs. Our hearts pounding, we darted down the hall, hoping to elude them before they reached Stoyian's floor.

The three of us scooted into the elevator and rode to the ground floor in dread the militia would be there waiting for us. Soon the door slid open and, seeing no one, we hurried outside, worried that Stoyian was at that very moment being arrested. As we reached the street, we separated without a word and met back at Veselin and Magda's. Later, we learned the militia had been after someone else. If they'd seen us, we would have been brought to the police station for interrogation.

These were a few of the many contacts we developed during our second year abroad. Upon reflection, on those trips we effectively organized a network which would soon see thousands and thousands of Bibles and other Christian literature delivered behind the Iron Curtain.

But Jeff and I were young and impatient then. About seven months into the season, a lack of funds, both DOHI's and ours, left us grounded at the Austrian base.

When we complained we weren't accomplishing much, Paul Popov urged us to have patience. "You can't run a mission like a business."

We wondered, why not? Goal-oriented creatures that we were, it seemed a terrible waste to spend the rest of the winter hibernating in Austria until funds came through in the spring. So we packed our bags and headed home early.

As our jet began its descent into Houston, stormy winds tossed it about, and lightning flashed through the cabin. The pilot attempted to lower the aircraft repeatedly, but it danced like a tin can in the wind. A frightened hush filled the plane.

I pleaded, "Lord, I'll do anything You want, if You'll get us down safely." I wondered, how many others were offering up similar prayers?

When we touched ground, everyone burst into applause. Praise God!

About a month later, Jeff and I were flying to Arkansas to speak at churches on behalf of DOHI. In Dallas, the airlines switched us to a nineteen-seater, which ran into tornadic winds. During the entire flight no one moved from their seats, not even the attendants. On the wild and scary ride, the plane seemed to plunge twenty feet and then zoom upward.

I never doubted God was in control, though I surmised if He didn't object to a tree falling on me, there was no telling what might happen next.

Yes, He promised, all things would work together for the good of those who love Him and are called according to His purposes, (Rom. 8:28). And He said, if we know how to give good gifts to those we love, how much more so our heavenly Father who loves us and showers us with His love accordingly, (Matt. 7:11).

This was all true and I didn't doubt it, but I was thinking about how the verse in Ecclesiastes says, "time and chance happeneth to them all," (9:11). My fear resulted in a crisis of faith, not in God but in my trust in His will being the absolute best for me.

I was so scared, I sang hymns and prayed aloud. And none of the other passengers asked me to pipe down.

As our plane reached Fort Smith, the pilot announced, "We are unable to land due to a tornado over the airport."

We flew back to Dallas in the same ghastly weather.

Afterward, every time I got on a plane, my hands grew clammy and a nauseous dread stirred within. How could I conquer my fear and trust God meant only good for me? Our mission work included frequent flights. Border searches through our vehicles, hidden compartments filled with Bibles, secret trysts and working with persecuted Christians beget a certain anxiety.

I prayed about my fear and confided in a few friends, asking them to pray with me. God heard our petition and delivered me. This doesn't mean I don't still have fears, but God gives me the courage to face them, while making abundantly clear His desire for everything in my life to work together for the good.

In my fear, I turned to the Lord in prayer and to His written Word, for strength. God never failed me. It wasn't always easy, but He met me where I stood every time, calling for me to come on up to higher ground.

God delivered me from a state of weakness and disbelief, and He keeps on delivering me. He has given us a way to overcome our fears through Him. Psalms 27 begins, "The Lord is my light and my salvation; whom shall I fear? The Lord is the strength of my life; of whom shall I be afraid?"

II Timothy 1:7 is another favorite scripture, "For God has not given us the spirit of fear; but of power, and of love, and a sound mind."

I was so wrapped up in my own fears, I didn't realize how terrified the other passengers were. Afterward, none of them were willing to get back on a plane.

No matter how big or little our fears, God will see us through. Scripture is an effective method to combat panic attacks and I have included some New Testament Scriptures on understanding and overcoming fear in the appendix.

THAT WINTER AT HOME, our hearts underwent an enormous change. Thus far, Jeff and I had made little mention to others of our work with DOHI. We were self-supporting missionaries. LaJewel Shrack, my Bible Study Fellowship (BSF) lecturer leader learned of our efforts abroad and asked if I would address a group of BSF leaders if she hosted a luncheon.

By then we had lots of slides from trips and a fairly accurate grasp of the situation confronting East European Christians. I spoke to the ladies, thrilled to find that their interest spiked questions. I gave everyone a copy of Haralan Popov's book, *Tortured For His Faith*.

LaJewel phoned after she read it and said, "I got down on my knees and cried, 'Oh God, I want to help. How I wish I had money to give Door of Hope International.'"

After several minutes of prayer, she heard God's soft answer, "You've got a mouth, use it."

LaJewel, one of the godliest women I've ever known, used her voice and influence to motivate hundreds of people to pray and give. Before her death in 1998 from an incurable brain tumor, she addressed hundreds of BSF women every Wednesday morning. As a Bible teacher, she was loved and respected by many. She used her influence to illustrate the plight of the persecuted church and DOHI's ministry behind the Iron Curtain. Soon I felt as if almost every woman there held us in prayer. It was a marvelous feeling to be covered in blessings through the generosity of others.

LaJewel gave me private lessons in homiletics, as well as advice and encouragement.

We usually spoke every Monday evening. She would share her one-sentence theme for the Wednesday BSF lecture so I could be praying. It usually began "cause the audience to . . ." and there would be a very specific verb there. She was a gifted and transparent speaker. Her lectures were captivating. Invariably, we would be on the phone close to an hour, talking about God and His mighty works.

JANUARY 1983, ON A TUESDAY night, Paul phoned. "Dad and I are going to be in Dallas next week and thought we'd drive down and see you both."

"Great, we'd love to have you." I arranged with Paul for us to ask several friends to our home the next Thursday to visit with Haralan.

Excited, I called LaJewel and a few others and invited them to our home to meet him.

The next morning at BSF, after a hurried, whispered consultation with me, LaJewel announced during her opening, "Haralan Popov will be in

71

Conroe next week. Wouldn't it be wonderful if our families and others could hear him speak? To do this we need a large facility. If anyone here can arrange the use of their church, please meet with me before the lecture." A number of pastors' wives attended BSF meetings.

Later when we trooped back into the sanctuary for the lecture, LaJewel invited all the ladies and their families to hear Haralan speak at the First Presbyterian Church the next Thursday.

Events had escalated beyond my wildest imagination. I phoned to tell Sharon, who arranged Haralan's itinerary from the DOHI Glendale office. Sharon said, "Haralan is already booked somewhere else on that date. Paul must have meant the Thursday after."

I cringed as I related the news to LaJewel who had to phone every discussion leader. They in turn had to call the members of their classes. LaJewel asked me to contact twenty-eight of the local congregations to request announcements be made for the benefit of those who could not be reached. I also stood outside First Presbyterian in the cold on the mistakenly appointed evening and explained to those who showed up what had occurred.

We all ate crow! Still God used our mistake to publicize the event.

Haralan finally arrived with Paul, who was trying to let me down easy so I wouldn't be disappointed by a small attendance. It was a cold rainy night and as we approached the church, it was already filling up. Soon the sanctuary was packed. This was the first occasion for Jeff and me to hear Haralan tell his story, and we were deeply moved. Teary-eyed, Paul spoke of being reunited with his dad after many years apart. It was a phenomenal evening.

Paul said the spontaneity of the event and the group's generosity was a great encouragement to his dad. The DOHI ministry was launched in Conroe that night and many of those who attended are still avid supporters.

18

Dramatic Events

AS WAS CUSTOMARY, in March we flew to California for a week-long courier training session. These seminars featured speakers from China, the U.S.S.R and Eastern Europe as well as the mission's US and Canadian personnel. The conference was held at the church of DOHI's European Director, Maria, whose congregation had generously offered their facilities.

Maria lived in Zweibrucken, Germany, most of the year. The tall attractive brunette and savvy Armenian-American was our immediate boss. She was also the former business manager of Door of Hope International's USA Glendale office. Back in Texas when we first met, Jeff and I had warmed to her easy laughter and personable style.

We were all asked to bring sleeping bags, since there weren't many beds. None of us minded, but Haralan was visibly upset. To him, sleeping on the floor conjured memories of cold, torturous prison cells. Despite our efforts to reassure him, he argued heatedly about the arrangements.

Jeff and I listened avidly, learning much from the roster of fascinating speakers: Haralan and Paul Popov; Russian Arkady Polishchuk, journalist, human rights advocate and author; Yanis Smit, Latvian pastor; Janis Karner, Estonian youth pastor; Dr. Zhang, Chinese pastor who spent eighteen years in prison for his faith; and many more.

Dr. Zhang recounted his long years of isolation and forced labor, shoveling huge drifts of human dung, a blessing. Because he stank, none of the other inmates wanted to be near him. This allowed him to pray without fear of reprisals.

Janis Karner spoke of how the KGB had tailed him everywhere he went. At one point there were thirty-five agents assigned to him. One afternoon, while out on church business he stopped at a market stand and bought two ice cream cones. He then turned and handed the second one to the chagrined KGB officer behind him.

The entire seminar was an opportunity to bond with those we would be working with on the mission field. Jeff and I were excited to be there and to learn, while meeting so many stalwart Christians.

———————

SOON IT WAS TIME to head overseas again. Like many travelers to Europe in the '80s, we flew KLM. Frequently, with the American airlines, there was the bother of changing planes and layovers in New York or Chicago, adding to our jet lag. To fly with British airlines usually meant lengthy hold-ups in London for baggage checks. Most of the other European airlines didn't fit our missionary purse.

I never complained about the delays in London. It was sensible and safer to let security do its job. Once at Heathrow, following hours of delays and security checks, we boarded and prepared for takeoff. Then an announcement came over the speakers: "All luggage is being unloaded from the aircraft for identification purposes. Everyone please exit the plane and identify your bags." We were told terrorists might have targeted a VIP who was on board. An individual of interest had checked his bags and failed to get on the flight. The police feared there might be a bomb among the luggage.

"Does this sort of thing occur often?" I asked an attendant.

He shook his head. "I've worked here fifteen years. It's the first time I've ever seen this happen."

No one minded. Instead, there was a sense of relief and the pervasive feeling, we'd experienced a near escape.

Amsterdam's Schiphol soon became our favorite airport for layovers.

They had a chapel for passengers. Comfortable seating throughout, good train and tram connections and lots of wonderful shops and boutiques repeatedly earned it the Airport of the Year Award in the '80s.

I often picked up small gifts at bargain prices in the basement grocery store. Jeff and I tried to bring annual tokens of appreciation to our friends, family and supporters. The list was extensive, and it was fun to search for a special gift for each person as we traveled.

The pressure of packing for six or more months was mind-boggling. Since the base vehicles were mostly American, we often had more car parts than clothes in our bags. Once we had a transmission shipped on our flight, then we drove it down to Spittal from Munich. Though it was indeed burdensome to ship parts and vehicles from the US to Europe, the benefits were sweeping. Jeff and I did much of the preplanning and coordination with couriers stateside. Files too sensitive to leave behind, journeyed back and forth with us.

Mission business, at times, demanded that we'd have to work our way down to Spittal or up to Amsterdam. Marvin and Nina, DOHI's *Russian Open Bible* translators, lived in Mainz. Jeff coordinated the conversion of DOHI's Bible projects from linotronic professional typesetting to simple PCs. Together he and Paul interviewed and set up oversight committees in Eastern Europe, drawing from various denominations for editorial and proofing purposes.

In conjunction with the publishing of DOHI's Bulgarian version of the *Open Bible Study Bible*, Jeff had asked Dr. Joseph Dimitrov, who taught New Testament Greek at the university in Brussels, to come on board, which he did. Visits with him and his lovely wife Yvetta and their two children were invariably delightful, as were those with Tarmo and Eila in Basel, Elisabeth and Dominic in Hirson, France, Daniel and Janine in Charleroi, Belgium, and the many with whom we labored in friendship.

Our couriers' successes were due in part to Paul's policy of not mixing nationalities. Americans were grouped together into like vehicles, which raised one less flag of suspicion at borders. Logically, it didn't make sense to customs officials to see an American young man, a middle-aged Dutchman and a Belgian female traveling in a motor home with Dutch plates. Yet some of the other missions operated in this manner. DOHI simply couldn't afford to take such risks.

Each spring, we felt a tremendous relief as the KLM 747 took flight from Houston Intercontinental to Amsterdam. If we'd forgotten anything, then so be it. In Holland, we would unwind and enjoy a few days of respite before driving on to the base in Austria.

Jeff and I arrived there in early April of 1983, eager to begin the courier season. Despite the warehouses of mission Bibles and RVs, we lacked the funds to finance enough trips to deliver all the Scriptures. Fuel was a major expense, running as high as $1,700 a trip, depending on which vehicle was driven. The RVs were large, and the Bibles were heavy; both of these factors drove up fuel costs.

Gradually, it became apparent, Jeff and I had a knack for Bible smuggling. We'd developed an innate sense of how to blend in and negotiate rendezvous, instincts some of those we worked with never acquired. Consequently, more and more of the direction of the Austrian base fell to us.

I'd like to share a bit about our lives before we knew Christ as our personal savior. As teenagers in the '60s, Jeff and I both regrettably fell into drugs for about a year and a half. There is a quality in our personalities that often causes us to go about whatever we are involved in with unreserved wholeheartedness. I'm afraid this is how we handled that brief period.

I was raised in Catholic schools until my parents divorced and remarried, and I later attended Bellaire High in Houston, where drugs were trendy. My universe went rapidly downhill. Soon I had left home and was selling drugs.

Meanwhile, Jeff, raised in the Baptist church, was attending Memorial High in Houston, following eight moves from Amarillo to Durango, then Tyler, Abilene and so on by his family to accommodate his dad's position with Amoco Oil Company. Like me, Jeff tried drugs in high school, left home and began dealing.

Jeff and I met through friends and eventually fell in love. God used circumstances and our love for each other to separate us from the drugs and the bad influences of that era. We married, and during our second term of college a young man witnessed to us on campus. As a result, we were saved and baptized in the Holy Spirit.

Christ's sacrifice for us on the cross buried our sins in the deepest part of the ocean, never to be remembered. His forgiveness made life worthwhile and exciting. Years later when we found ourselves smuggling Bibles in Eastern Europe, the realization dawned—God had taken the vilest part of our lives, polished it for His use and turned it into something beautiful.

There was new life in Christ. Instead of making cocaine runs, we were delivering God's Word into the hands of Christians. We'd never been happier, despite the challenges and frustrations of missionary work.

Midsummer of 1983, Paul invited us to attend DOHI's international board meeting, which was being held that year in nearby Seeboden, Austria. Initially, it was exciting, getting acquainted with the directors from various countries and learning the inner workings of the mission. By the end of the week, however, a heavy inconsolable despair permeated my spirit.

This was our third summer ministering to brave Christians who smiled amid tears of oppression and persecution. Each cancelled trip earlier in the spring had meant fewer Bibles and fewer promises kept, a failure we took personally. Jeff and I were consumed with thoughts of how to get more Scriptures behind the Iron Curtain. It was what we were about then, our very heartbeat.

As I listened to the directors put together an international budget for the next year, it became clear distribution was not a priority. Translation and printing was their primary focus. I understood how necessary these were, but it seemed to me, if we couldn't afford to deliver the Bibles we had, what was the point of filling warehouses with more? Admittedly, this was shortsighted, yet God used my single-mindedness.

As the week marched on, the stark reality set in, we would not be moving a great number of Bibles. The funds simply weren't there. I thought of the many Christians we'd befriended in Eastern Europe and the thousands and thousands of others desperately wanting a Bible of their own to read, and I wanted to cry. Without funds how were we going to transport those in the warehouses to them?

A sob shook me, and I struggled to suppress it. The harder I tried, the more my tears fell. I was mortified as others turned to stare at me, wondering what was wrong. I couldn't stop crying. I can't remember if I rushed out of the room or simply sat there and tried to regain control. I couldn't leave the premises because we were scheduled to show slides and give a report on the Austrian base's operations.

Afterward, Paul asked me what was wrong. A few of the other directors paused to listen as I said, "We have warehouses full of Bibles and you're printing and translating more when the mission doesn't have enough gas money to distribute those it already has."

Paul, who had a sincere empathy for the courier ministry, was caught in the middle. "Door of Hope International has traditionally been a Bible translating and printing mission. I can't see why we should change that." Paul had a responsibility to fund the projects the mission had begun. Teams were translating *The Thomas Nelson Open Bible* into Romanian, Russian and Bulgarian as well as a song book and *The Hailey's Handbook* into Romanian and a number of other ongoing projects. Most of the translators lived in the West and their salaries drew a substantial part of the budget, along with the many associated costs of printing and smuggling proofs in and out of Eastern Europe.

On the other hand, Jeff and I had been asked by Paul, on behalf of the mission, to travel to Europe for a purpose. We had taken the commission fully to heart and in so doing found it difficult to be content to accomplish so little.

Benjamin Cocar, a pastor in Romania, had told us of a missionary who came now and then to see him. Each visit, the man would spend about $20 on him. On one trip, the man confessed, his organization couldn't afford to do more. This missionary felt guilty because he had spent hundreds of dollars traveling and staying in nice hotels, then had so little to give.

Door of Hope International certainly didn't operate this way. Still, Jeff and I were compelled to be productive to justify our time in Europe. Our impatience and youth were perhaps too apparent.

Still God used these, just as He used my tears that day as various DOHI European directors were made more personally aware of the Bible couriers' ministry and the necessity of funding such trips. Elisabeth, DOHI/France's director, came up to me after Paul and I spoke and asked why I was so upset. When I explained, her interest was kindled, and she offered to send money from their budget's discretionary funds. In turn, she requested we speak of our courier work at their annual Christian Conference in Hirson later in the fall. France's funding of the Austrian base helped tremendously.

Miraculously, DOHI directors, Phil Streeter from England and Daniel Voumard, from Belgium offered assistance as well. They also requested that Jeff and I speak on behalf of Door of Hope International in their respective countries. Paul was also pleased because their funding aided a project close to his heart without adding undue strain to the US or international budgets.

19

Representing DOHI

IN THE FALL, I traveled to France alone, pausing briefly in Germany's Black Forest region to see Tarmo and Eila. This dedicated and seasoned missionary couple was such an encouragement to Jeff and me, always willing to offer help and counsel if needed. I visited with these dear friends in their home. Then we enjoyed lunch in nearby Basil where I boarded an express train scheduled to arrive in Hirson late that afternoon.

Darkness descended and I was still traveling. It was an eerie feeling. No one seemed to speak English, and I was reluctant to try German. The locomotive stopped in the countryside, and with no idea where we were, I worried I was on the wrong train. Eventually, the train moved on and at about half past midnight chugged into Hirson. Elisabeth, a petite, sun-kissed blonde, met me and drove me to her home where I fell into bed, exhausted.

Morning came too soon. In her cheery red and white tiled kitchen, Elisabeth pointed to the cereal and bowls on the table and said in her delightful French accent, "Everything you need should be here. The children are in the car, waiting for me to drive them to school. Help yourself to coffee."

Half asleep, I spotted a pot of coffee but nothing to pour it in. "Where are the cups?"

She gestured toward the bowls on the table. "Here."

I glanced around. "Where?"

A hint of impatience crept into her voice. "Right here."

Evidently, we weren't communicating. "Something to drink from." I mimicked lifting a cup to my lips.

"Americans," she muttered, then reached into the cabinet, drew out a cup and saucer and set them on the table. Elisabeth dashed out the door calling, "I'll be back soon."

Mystified by her reaction, I sat enjoying the French roast and the quiet time to myself until her return.

After lunch, she drove us to a large older chateau which her parents had purchased and transformed into a Christian Conference Center. Her father was a pastor and many of his friends and other Christians had traveled from different regions of the country for the weekend.

Everyone greeted me with a kiss on each cheek, while shaking my hand and saying, "*Bonjour.*" I would like to say we visited, though invariably where there are three or more French gathered, they soon lapse into their native tongue.

At the evening service, Elisabeth interpreted as I spoke and showed a slide presentation on the courier ministry and its needs. The crowd responded generously.

Though one could easily envision the chateau's former grandeur and dream of days gone by, the reality paled. That night, in an effort to fight off the damp chill, I slept in my nightgown, bathrobe, sweater and two pairs of socks.

The next morning, everyone gathered at long tables in the dining room for breakfast. To my surprise, I was the guest of honor. The waiter served me first, pouring java into a large, deep bowl. The others watched me expectantly. I looked around, feeling gauche and clueless as to how to handle a cup of coffee the size of a mixing bowl.

Fortunately, a kind pastor's wife seated on my right understood my dilemma. She signaled the waiter to fill the rest of the bowl with hot milk. Then I mimicked her, and delicately picked up the bowl with two fingers and sipped, as if I were drinking from the finest Wedgwood rather than a porcelain bowl that outdid any Texas-size cup I'd ever seen. The group seemed to breathe a sigh of relief, as did I, and the waiters moved to serve others, deflecting attention from me.

Sunday services followed, then lunch. Daniel Voumard arrived in the afternoon to drive me to Belgium. His accent, diplomacy and understated wit, coupled with his sparkling dark brown eyes, conjured Agatha Christie's *Hercule Poirot.*

Daniel and his wife Janine soon became dear friends and allies in our missionary endeavors. As I walked into the church that his father, a missionary from Switzerland, had founded and still pastored, I was enveloped by its warmth. They greeted me with three rapid kisses on my cheeks instead of the French two, amid exclamations of "*Ça va, ça va.*"

I spoke to the congregation about the Suffering Church and our efforts to bring the people Bibles. Daniel translated. As I revealed my heart, I sensed the congregation's growing excitement.

Afterward, we learned the trains and planes in Belgium were on strike. Daniel and Janine drove me across the border to Aachen, Germany. I boarded a train there around 10:00 p.m., traveling through Köln and arriving in Frankfurt station about one in the morning. I took in the seedy characters hanging around and worried about the thousands of dollars' worth of donated French and Belgium *francs* in my purse.

At the information booth, I asked for a hotel recommendation, then caught a cab out front. The young German driver kept glancing at me in the rearview mirror. Finally, he asked, "*Fraulein, verstehen Sie diese* hotel is a flop house for whores?"

I was still dressed in my Sunday church clothes. Shocked and embarrassed, I assured him, "No. I didn't know."

"*Ich habe das gedacht.* You don't look like that sort of woman." He suggested a nice, reasonably priced hotel and drove me there. Thank the Lord!

The next day I was blessed to book a flight to Austria, since it was a national holiday. There were so many religious days when all businesses ground to a halt, Jeff often teased, "What, is Mary ascending again?"

I gathered my belongings and stepped out to meet the taxi arranged to take me to the airport. The maid called to me, *"Fraulein, ein moment, bitter. Sie haben Ihre Kleid vergessen."* She ran and handed me one of my favorite dresses I'd left in the room. God's care was apparent in the smallest details.

Wonderful seeds were planted at those two meetings. Daniel phoned to tell us a woman in his church had donated $25,000 toward a new RV for Bible smuggling. Delighted at the news, I danced around the kitchen, praising God. Later that summer Elisabeth accompanied us on a courier trip and became a strong advocate of the courier ministry, as did Daniel, his sister in Switzerland and Phil from England, all DOHI directors. In return, each fall we devoted about six weeks to the whirlwind itineraries they set up in their respective countries. God had graciously provided strong support close to the Austrian base. We were bursting with excitement at His many blessings.

One custom that I had difficulty adjusting to was eating with my fork in the left hand and the knife in the right. So successful was my indoctrination as a child, that the mere thought of lifting my fork to my mouth overhand left me feeling like a barbarian. To this day, I've never understood how Americans came to eat so differently from the rest of the world. Nevertheless, after about a year, I knew I had to change or risk offending my hosts.

Once we grew conditioned to the European method, I found it easier and more practical than I would have ever imagined. Jeff and I often revert to this style when we're alone because of its convenience.

After five or six years, I became rather adept. Yet I also noted slight nuances in the table manners of various European countries. One fall, we were in Brussels at a dinner with a large group, following a church meeting. As we continued to eat, I noticed some variations from the Austrian style Jeff and I employed. I wondered if these minor differences might seem ill-mannered to others. Midway through the meal I decided to switch to the American method, wanting to avoid any offensive errors.

Several minutes later, our host rose in anger. "The American feels she is too good to eat like the rest of us."

I wanted to disappear. With an apology, I switched my knife and fork to opposite hands and swallowed a bite, though the food seemed to stick in my throat. Any explanations seemed trite in the midst of his ill-humored comments.

After this experience, I left the nuances of European table manners to others. Thankfully, on the numerous occasions we were invited to dinner at the homes of friends and acquaintances in Belgium and other countries, this was the single occasion when we were not treated with warm hospitality and kindness.

ONE AUTUMN IN CHARLEROI, BELGIUM, I determined to mark our wedding anniversary. For several years running, the European offices had booked us for church services in either France or Belgium on the occasion. I asked the couple we were staying with to keep that night free. It wasn't possible. Still at our request, Daniel arranged a hotel stay so we could go out to dinner before the meeting and celebrate.

Naturally, our room had to be near the church. We barely had time to walk around the corner to McDonald's in downtown Charleroi. There went my visions of an elegant dinner. After the service, we returned to our room and decided to watch a movie in honor of the occasion. The only one on was a depressing German nuclear war flick, which Jeff got caught up in. Finally, it was over, and we were ready to snuggle into bed. Whoosh! Our bodies sank almost to the floor in the soft feathery mattress. To save our backs, Jeff wrestled it onto the carpet.

The night seemed far from special. Obviously, my plans hadn't concurred with God's, and I felt selfish to have disrupted everyone else's. With a sigh, I switched off the light and tried to vanquish the end-of-the-world images haunting me in this strange and far from comfortable hotel room.

The night was reminiscent of another evening in London. Phil Streeter had booked us for several weeks of meetings in England. Initially, we visited with him and his wife Diane in Hornchurch and reviewed the itinerary. "After the tour, Diane wants you to come back and stay here your last night before heading on to Austria," Phil said.

I would have enjoyed visiting, but my heart was set on going to the theater. "Thank you, but we've already made plans. It's our only free night in London."

The tour went well. Our days were delightfully free to sightsee. We walked the chalk-white cliffs of Dover, spent hours and hours in the British Museum, roamed the ancient streets of Cirencester. In Wales, we were close enough to stop off for an afternoon in Chester, strolling about Roman walls and arches built centuries ago. I was also excited to visit the Wedgewood factory and check on my china pattern.

The autumn breezes were chilly. I wore two pairs of thick wool socks, which entailed buying shoes a size larger so my feet and the socks would fit. Wool prices were so reasonable, I bought a few berets, a scarf and extra sweaters to wear beneath my coat.

Jeff and I stayed mostly in the homes of DOHI supporters who had arranged the meetings through Phil. Though for about a week in Cirencester we lived in the officers' military quarters. The accommodations were cold but the food marvelous. We bought an electric space heater for the spacious but sparse room and bath.

Meals were served in a formal paneled dining room with fine china, silver and crystal. Since our schedule did not coincide with that of the officers, we were served dinner earlier. Still, it was mandatory to dress for meals. It was a pleasant contrast to the months of roughing it in Eastern Europe. A waiter stood at our elbows in solitary state, serving up scrumptious courses, which left us feeling as if we'd landed in a bit of heaven.

As planned, we bought tickets to the theater in London and sat through a cold, modernistic play that neither of us enjoyed. I have always regretted the missed opportunity to be with Diane. I can still see us seated in the warmth of her home, laughing and talking. If I could choose again, it would be the substance of friendship rather than the mere glibness of being able to say, "Oh, we went to the theater in London and saw . . . let me see, what was that play?"

Anxious to be back home in Austria, we drove to Dover after the theater to catch the ferry to Calais. The next evening a hurricane whipped through Dover, causing much destruction. If we hadn't driven on, we would have been there. I was thankful for God's protection on our journey.

20

Courier Directors

THE WINTER OF 1984, Maria resigned. Jeff and I were appointed co-directors of Door of Hope International's literature distribution into Eastern Europe. We were eager to develop and implement an expanded courier program. For the annual missionary training conference, we signed up nurses, doctors, bankers, brokers, carpenters, mechanics, and housewives who were willing to spend their vacations smuggling Bibles. They paid their own trip expenses, including the cost of driving the RVs into Eastern Europe and back, which solved our fuel cost crunch.

Those applying to be DOHI missionaries, both long and short term, went through an application screening process which included resumes, references and various checks prior to attending these seminars. Near the end of each conference Paul, Jeff and I interviewed participants, working out the times and assignments for those who were accepted.

One spring, Steve, a pastor from California, and his wife flew into Houston to attend a DOHI Courier Seminar at the Marriott. He was amazed at the in-depth training he received. With another mission often confused with Door of Hope International, he said, his training had consisted of ten minutes of instruction before he drove off with a mixed team of volunteers to deliver smuggled Bibles.

God blessed us with many wonderful and dedicated couriers who returned annually. Some, like John and Charlene, newlyweds when we first interviewed them, eventually became full-time missionaries. Every other spring it seemed John and his wife arrived with another child in tow. This was a great cover, however it must have taken immense faith on both their parts.

John was a business owner with a large heart for the Lord. Whatever the task, he'd smile and give it his best effort. He became a fulltime missionary in Ohrid, Macedonia, and Albania, active in church planting, evangelism and humanitarian assistance in Kosovo.

Then there was the Tallahassee bunch. Mike T and his friend Mike M, who both worked in the technology field, joined up one summer. They returned annually and recruited more members from their church. Lisa B, a former political appointee with the Reagan Administration who had worked as a senior writer/editor at the US Department of Education, was public relations director with the Florida Chamber of Commerce, when she and her friend Ellen, a nurse, joined the team. Mike T and Ellen fell in love on the mission field, were married and had several children. Lisa went on to direct a refugee center in Croatia for seven years and has now returned to the States.

We were also blessed with couriers from Jackson, Mississippi, thanks to Shirley and Ted W. Ted, a banker, had developed an extensive ministry distributing Bibles on foreign vessels docking at US ports.

I remember interviewing them at a missionary conference in California. Ted voiced his doubts about the cost and time effectiveness of Bible smuggling. When Ted learned he could deliver from 650 to five thousand Bibles into Eastern Europe in one short two-week vacation, he got excited. He and his wife became couriers and brought others from their church into the work. They remained active, helping to print and distribute Bibles and build churches abroad until they passed away.

These are just a few of the many who came—from New York, New Jersey, Michigan, California, Oregon, Texas, Florida and more. It would take another book to name them all and tell their stories. God brought them, weaving a cohesive family and team with one compelling burden—to deliver

Bibles. Soon we had so many trips occurring that our prayers included the need for more RVs.

Back home in Texas, LaJewel and I mapped out a prayer strategy for the development of the Austrian base and its couriers. As we headed to Europe each year, BSF leaders, members and friends helped in creative and unusual ways. They provided free shipping for needed items such as tires, darkening film to use on the windows to improve the security of mission vehicles, and office chairs and desks for the new Texas office, which had now become a necessity. LaJewel and close BSF friends, Sue Phillips, Dorothy Vercellino, and Dilly Anderson were always there for us, praying and toiling behind the scenes to garner support for the ministry.

BSF husbands joined in as well. Our story wouldn't be complete without the mention of Willie Vercellino, Jack Phillips, Bill Shrack, Nita Beth and John Mitchell, and John and Ann Nelson whom God used in immeasurable ways to further our work behind the Iron Curtain. Some of these precious friends have since passed away, but they continue to be in our hearts and memories.

I was in the grocery store one spring getting ready to leave for Europe, when I ran into a BSF friend, Nora Mae Odom. She smiled her big heartwarming smile and handed me a check for $200.00. "This is for you and Jeff," she said. "I don't care about a tax deduction. I want you to be able to use the money now for whatever you might need personally."

Dazed, grateful and slightly embarrassed, I accepted our first donation. The second one came as I was leaving a BSF meeting and Dorothy Vercellino handed me a sizable check.

At some point, Jeff and I put our home on the market with the idea we would donate the proceeds from the sale to Door of Hope International. It was the '80s though and real estate was not selling. I think God protected us in our zeal, because He knew we needed a home of our own to return to.

As the work grew abroad, our winters stateside were taken up with organizing for the summer months. Door of Hope International's missionary conferences moved to the Houston area, which was more centrally located. We experimented with Tallahassee and even tried hosting the event in Los Angeles again, but the seminars in Houston were more heavily attended by volunteers from across America.

The California office asked me to arrange an itinerary for Haralan in our area since Conroe now had so many DOHI supporters. I said yes, though I didn't have a clue how to accomplish this. Jeff's mother hosted a luncheon and LaJewel and Sue Phillips shared what DOHI meant to them. I invited those present to pray about approaching their pastors on behalf of the mission. Soon we had Haralan booked solid for a month of meetings to coincide with our training event.

Participants paid their own hotel and travel expenses. And with much prayer, I arranged for other speakers throughout the conference to speak in area churches on Sunday mornings. It was hectic but the offerings covered their airfare, hotel and food throughout the seminar, and they had such wonderful testimonies to share of God's work in Eastern Europe. Local friends drove them while we concluded the meetings and interviewing process.

So much effort went into these events. Sharon Davis, our full-time volunteer secretary in Conroe, and Liz Heron, our accountant were invaluable. These two handled so many details that we'll forever be thankful to them, and their families for sharing them. Many others assisted, and we remember them as well with thanksgiving in our hearts for making a difficult job easier.

Haralan usually stayed with Jeff's parents, Jim and Elaine Kendrick, who actively supported our ministry in myriad ways. We'll always be grateful to them. They hosted wonderful annual dinners for our supporters. Jim once drove one of the vehicles we purchased in Texas all the way to the port in North Carolina. It was shipped from there to Amsterdam for the mission's use in the courier ministry. On another occasion, he drove my car from Burbank to Conroe while I flew. Likewise, our former next-door neighbors and dear friends Diane and Bill Burnich handled enough details for us through the years to be nominated for sainthood.

Those days we spent with Haralan were special as well. Since I often drove him to his engagements, I heard him speak again and again, and I was always touched. On each occasion it was as if I were hearing him for the first time.

21

The Nolan Family

THE AUSTRIAN BASE GREW into a lively bustling place with teams flying in and out. Couriers like Mark and Holly from New Jersey; Jo Ann, Bob and their friends from Michigan; Tito, Tony and their many California and Oregon pals; the Nolans, Burniches and others from Conroe and various cities volunteered. With rare exceptions, everyone pitched in with a will to serve. Meals had to be prepared for large groups, and laundry and cleaning were ongoing. Those who failed to adapt were not invited back. Our goals were too serious for those who were not contributing in earnest.

A typical day began with breakfast, followed by group devotions with rotating leaders. At 9:00 a.m. work commenced. Paul Aston, an Idaho mechanic, came one summer as a missionary and stayed. With Jeff's oversight and many assistants, Paul ran the garages. He remained throughout the year, helping to open and close the base in the spring and fall.

Humor and a shared sense of adventure helped everyone deal with the inherent stress. When our friends Jill and Conrad Nolan arrived with their children, Ben, age seven, and Michelle, age five, their courage and faith were tested. Despite a natural curiosity, the details of Bible smuggling had to be kept from the young. Ben had a new camera and snapped pictures as if he were PR man of the year.

Whenever possible, we gave new arrivals the local tour and a few days to acclimate. Like most, the Nolans' tour opened with the breathtaking eight-minute drive up into the densely forested Alps. The road cut through massive rocks and mountains, curling alongside the gushing river, streams and waterfalls where each summer Europe's international kayak races were held. A sentry amid the serene foothills, the church spire towered above the village of Seeboden and its azure lake.

A few kilometers away, the rippling waters of Lake Millstatt hugged the Alpine terrain, stretching for miles. A fifteen-minute tour of the area was sure to impress new recruits. Even, I couldn't stifle a sigh of pleasure at such exquisite beauty, despite having seen it often. There are many places around the world where our base might have been located—yet God blessed us with the beauty of the state of Carinthia in Southern Austria.

We led the group through painted yellow archways a foot thick, dating back to AD 700 – 800. The path led to an old monastery built in the 1200s where we paused to view faded ancient paintings on the outer courtyard walls. Then we strolled around a huge one thousand-year-old linden tree.

Our sightseeing frequently ended with strudel and coffee by the lake or in one of the area castles. In Spittal, the *Schloss Porcia*, an Italian Renaissance castle built in the fifteenth century, was a favorite. It hosted a myriad of musical events and plays, which included international choir competitions. Jill exclaimed, "The castle is unlike anything I've ever seen. It's so immense, ornate and ancient. I felt like I was in a different era."

On the Nolans' first night, we went to *Schloss Berg*, a medieval fortress in Seeboden. Inside, the stone walls were illuminated by candlelight and decorated with ancient armor that fascinated Ben in particular. He was quite precocious. At his parents' request, as we sat around an aged wooden table, Ben recited the entire Gettysburg address word for word. We cheered him on.

It soon became apparent, Ben's curiosity might be a problem. The base garage was strictly off limits. Still, he managed to stumble in when his dad and some of the men were loading the secret compartments. He was promptly sent out in the hope he couldn't possibly guess what was going on.

The opposite of her serious and intrepid brother, Michelle was a tease. At breakfast, she would whisper "Jeana," repeating my name in a singsong voice, soft enough for no one else to notice but precisely loud enough to keep me on edge. No one except the Nolans, who were from our hometown, knew our real names. Michelle was too young to understand how perilous the game she played was. They were great kids, however they kept us alert.

Eventually however, everything was in readiness. The Nolan family climbed into the Diamond RV and headed for the Romanian border. Jeff and I left by car, entering the country from another spot where we met up with a number of arriving teams and set about distributing the Bibles they carried.

When our rendezvous time with Conrad and Jill came and they didn't appear, we waited anxiously, then called the base, using a prearranged code. We learned they had been turned back. The Romanian border guards had suspected the camper carried Bibles and drilled into the walls. Jill and Conrad were fairly shaken.

Searches were difficult for couriers and they knew when customs officials brought out drills, hammers and saws, trouble was decidedly on the horizon. Jill and Conrad bombarded heaven with prayers and pleas, trying to look as innocent and outraged as possible, while willing their fear to disappear.

An officer pointed to a spot on the camper wall and barked out an order.

The Nolan family heard the buzz of the drill as seconds crawled past, stretching into long minutes of monstrous pressure. When the first drill bit was pulled back wrapped with pink cotton candy like insulation, a surge of relief washed over them. And the next drilling was the same . . . and the next. They prayed, "Please God, don't let them hit paper." The guards drilled more places, missing again and again.

Although Romanian customs didn't find anything, the authorities remained suspicious and refused them entry into the country. Later, it was discovered the officials had drilled right between two rows of Bibles. Praise the Lord for His mighty deliverance!

Jill and Conrad drove into Yugoslavia and phoned the base for instructions about what to do next. It must have been with enormous unease that they received our message to drive up through Hungary and try to enter Romania through a different border. They endured another long search which, though expected, was nonetheless nerve-racking, especially on the heels of their previous attempt. Eventually, they were allowed into Romania and were deeply touched to see the Christians' joy at receiving the Bibles they had brought.

At the conclusion of their trip, we all rendezvoused at the Austrian base. Conrad and his family traveled, next, to Bulgaria in the fifth wheel. We met them at the campground there. While Jeff helped them unload, I cooked spaghetti for Ben and Michelle in the Diamond. My object was to keep the children occupied, ensuring they didn't stumble into the other RV while the Bibles were being unloaded. I stood at the camper stove.

Ben said, "We had a pretty long border search."

Michelle agreed, "Those guards were scary." She looked up at me. "How did your crossing go?"

"Fine," I reassured her. "Nothing unusual."

They began to compare the different entry points they'd been through. In a few short weeks, Ben and Michelle had passed through three Yugoslavian borders, as many Romanian, two Hungarian and one Bulgarian.

I gazed at their intent faces and wondered how many kids sat around discussing border crossings.

Ben cleared his throat and stared at me intently. "What are my dad and Jeff doing?"

"They're simply taking care of some things, and remember it's Phillip not Jeff."

"It's just us." He glanced outside, scanning the area as if to make sure no one was listening. A curious determination crept into his gaze. "They're unpacking Bibles, aren't they? That's what everyone was doing in the garage in Austria, wasn't it? Hiding Bibles?"

With a stern look, I ladled spaghetti onto their plates. "Would you two quit worrying and just eat dinner? Try to enjoy your vacation."

At their home in Conroe, Ben and Michelle learned the truth. These days, both are strong adult Christians actively involved in missions.

22

Benjamin and Danielle

GOD'S GRACE WITH US was the recurrent theme on each and every trip. Though the couriers' experiences made interesting stories, the Christians receiving the Bibles faced much more danger. They distributed the Bibles in an environment hostile to their very existence. These brothers' and sisters' faith and hunger for God's Word inspired us to new levels of service. And chief among these were the Cocars.

The twinkle in Pastor Benjamin Cocar's eyes and his earnest charm drew people to him. He and his wife Danielle and their young son Ray, now grown, were radiant beacons in a bleak era of Romania's history. Her father and Benjamin co-pastored the most active church in the city of Medias. They endured the constant threat of arrest, suffering dangerous and routine interrogations. When Benjamin left for these sessions, Danielle never knew if he would return. Sometimes Christians ostensibly vanished. Yet in the midst of travail and turmoil, their joy and devotion in the Lord spilled over, bringing hundreds to know Christ.

I remember crossing the drive to enter the cool shady courtyard of their home many an afternoon and evening. Danielle's parents lived with them. As soon as Jeff and I arrived, they started cooking. We sat in the living room and visited with Benjamin while Danielle and her mother prepared wonderful meals. When the food was ready, everyone gathered in the dining room and ate. Benjamin and Danielle, who spoke excellent English, regaled us with stories of their lives, church and country.

Their home was a welcoming sanctuary, and we enjoyed a deep kinship with this couple. To save money, Jeff and I mostly slept in campgrounds. Often we opened a can of vegetables while driving and ate without stopping. Frequently, we drove as many as seventy hours a week. Most of our visits were at night, and by morning we might be in another town or country.

The campground in nearby Sibiu was relatively nice, compared to others. To avoid raising red flags, we stayed some distance from our contacts. Thus, when Jeff and I delivered Bibles to Medias we usually slept in Sighisoara. The site was little more than a pasture with one cold, dirty, mosquito-filled shower. Worse, there was no hot water. I remember it well, showering in the freezing water, swatting at mosquitos all the while.

In particular, I recall one cold and rainy spring. We slept in a pop-up tent that had developed a leak, and the downpour soaked our clothes and bedding, leaving us chilled and miserable. That afternoon in Medias, Benjamin and Danielle handed me a wrapped gift. I opened it to discover a lovely Romanian peasant blouse—exactly what I needed, and they had no definite idea when we would be coming. They were God's instruments of grace to us. Their many kindnesses will never be forgotten.

Benjamin told us of an incident that occurred on his journey home following a late-night rendezvous with us. We'd met on some dark shadowy street and loaded Benjamin's trunk until the rear of his beige Lada slumped beneath the weight of Bibles. The back and front passenger's seats were similarly filled. As he drove off, the Lada seemed to groan under its burden.

"I never stopped praying the entire trip home," Benjamin said. "Out on the highway there was an accident and the police waved a wand for me to stop. I pulled up ahead so the militia couldn't see inside, then ran back a few yards to where the group stood.

"One of the policemen motioned toward a drunk man who had been injured in the collision. 'You, get him to the hospital!'"

Benjamin continued. "I knew if I refused they would interrogate me and search the car. So I agreed and assisted the man to my Lada, barely visible in the black night. Quickly, I shoved the hurt man into the back seat on top of the Bibles, closing the door before he could object. Then I rammed the car into gear and took off, all the while praying. I discovered the man's tongue had been nearly cut in half, making it impossible for him to talk, a miracle. He couldn't report the Bibles. I dropped him off at the hospital without anyone recognizing me. Later, my wife and I praised God for His provision and for bringing me home safely with the Bibles."

Despite the poverty in Romania and their personal struggle to survive, Benjamin and Danielle were keen to make our lives easier. Jeff had mentioned he was searching for a leather passport wallet like one he'd bought a few years earlier in Bucharest. On our next visit, Benjamin and Danielle presented him with an entire stack of these wallets, which they had gone to the trouble and expense of finding and buying.

One spring, Paul Popov asked Jeff and me to help arrange an itinerary for the Continental Singers across Eastern Europe. Excited about the upcoming performance in Sibiu, Benjamin's congregation wanted to express their thanks to the singers in a tangible manner. So, the congregants carved and stained one hundred-fifty wooden plates, depicting their church in Medias. Sadly, the Continental Singers came but the authorities refused to allow them to sing in Medias as a punishment to Benjamin and the church members. Benjamin was crushed but he took the news with a woeful smile, offering us one of the plates as a gift.

The plate hangs in my home, a reminder of prayerful late-night rendezvous on forgotten highways where Bibles changed hands, our trunk to his, and of warm enchanted visits and meals in their home.

Jeff and I would exclaim, "*Foarte bine*," the Romanian words for very good, or "*Multumesc,*" which means thank you, and they would smile and try to teach us a new word or phrase, their hearts laid bare before us.

Perhaps, one of their greatest gifts was the ability to trust God enough to lay themselves open to ridicule, arrest, prison and even death. They did this in Romania where people were starving in a nation once considered the breadbasket of Europe. Flour was rationed monthly, one-quarter kilo per family. Milk was a black-market item few could afford. Soap, tooth-brushes, fresh produce, shoes, gasoline, electricity and other goods were equally difficult to obtain.

On one trip, I lost my toothbrush and, after days of searching during stops in various cities, the only one I found to buy was a used one at the Bucharest Hotel Intercontinental at a dollar shop designed for Western tourists. Most people washed their clothes in bathtubs and these were the Romanian educated elite who knew more about philosophy, literature, art and physics than I could ever aspire to know.

Except for the mountainous region of Moldavia, the terrain was remi-niscent of Southeast Texas, with lots of rain, humidity, hot sunny summer days and green landscapes. The campground on the outskirts of Sibiu could have been set in the pasture beyond my own backyard in Conroe, so close was the resemblance, overgrown grass fields and a tall canopy of trees. The likeness ended there.

In the evening, the town's people walked, drove or rode the tram to the Sibiu campground for entertainment. The main attraction was a rubber ball loosely tied to a backboard set on a pole. Everyone lined up for their chance to pay and punch the ball. Disco music blared throughout the camp until two or three in the morning. And armed soldiers patrolled the area on foot.

Many a sweltering night, I lay in our popup tent, trying to tune out the noise, praying for contentment and sleep. God always answered those prayers. Those experiences taught me to be thankful for a clean hot shower at the end of a long day. In my discomfort, I was reminded of those less fortunate. Praise our God. He is there for each of us regardless of our nationality or circumstances.

One afternoon, Benjamin confided, "It breaks my heart to see my peo-ple reduced to begging. If I stop for a train or a traffic light, kids surround the car, pleading for food. Milk is only sold on the black market to those with enough money to pay. How are our children to survive? What is to become of our nation?"

Benjamin continued, "During the summer when the corn is harvested, the militia barricade the streets and check all our cars for hidden corn kernels. In the capital Bucharest, the people are searched as they leave to prevent them from smuggling food to the surrounding cities. The capital has more supplies than the rest of the country."

In Romania, traffic moved slowly, pedestrians almost as numerous as the cars. Gypsy girls and boys, their faces pinched with hunger, sat in the back of horse-drawn wagons. Peasant women swung sickles along the roadsides, harvesting weeds to feed their animals. Old men carried huge mounds of hay on their backs, the load covering all but their legs as they walked. Farmers and factory workers spilled onto the highways and avenues, forcing traffic to halt. They were intent on using their streets, despite whatever other freedoms Ceausescu's brutal dictatorship had usurped.

Once, Jeff and I were stopped by the police for an imaginary traffic offense and charged an exorbitant fine. Instead of demanding payment, the officers pointed to their mouths and bellies, signaling food would suffice. I scrounged a can of tuna from a sack in the car, and they left happy. Militia performing spot checks in the countryside have flagged us down and demanded food. And as we approached the border, the first level of guards pleaded for a banana or an apple to feed their children.

Gasoline lines were enormous, like nothing the West has experienced, stretching for blocks and miles. Romanians were only allowed to purchase fuel on certain days. The acute shortage caused DOHI couriers problems as well. On dozens of trips, we drove from town to town, stopping at gas stations to learn they had no fuel to sell. If we found a station with gasoline or diesel, they often had no electricity to pump it.

It was not uncommon for electricity to be rationed. Two days on and two days off was routinely practiced. For families crowded into blocks of apartment flats with no other source of heat, winter could be excruciating. Our dear friends Stefan and Carmen burnt their furniture one winter to protect their children from illness.

Ceausescu, an uneducated shoemaker with only four years of elementary school, rose to power with the Communists' assistance. He became the party leader in 1965 and the nominal head of state in '67. He served as Romania's president from 1974–1989 in a position he created for himself by converting his post as president of the state council to a full-fledged presidency. Ceausescu borrowed heavily from the West to build factories throughout the country. There were few goods to produce in these plants, and the massive project was a huge failure.

At Ceausescu's insistence, most of Romania's goods were exported and the income reserved to pay its tremendous debt. The people starved, while the president's family and the select few enjoying the nation's abundance lived like kings.

As happens in such societies, the black market flourished, and corruption grew. One day, Jeff and I were in the Citroën with the gas gauge nearing empty. We had two teams in Bible-laden RVs parked on the side of the highway, out of fuel. We scouted for miles through various cities, but there was either no fuel available or no electricity to pump it. Rain drizzled and threatened to pour throughout the gray, overcast day.

Finally, we made contact with some black marketeers and met them at the garbage dump. They had a barrel of fuel, and we bought enough for our car and the RVs. Later, when we asked Benjamin about this, he said, "The people work for almost nothing. Any progress merely fattens Ceausescu's purse. The farmer is forced to plow his family's fields, which he no longer owns, and watch his crops exported to others while his family starves. He may look the other way when the tractor's fuel is stolen or sell it himself to feed his little ones. It's the same at construction sites, hotels, almost anywhere you go. Romanians are desperate, and Ceausescu is much hated."

To counter his unpopularity, Ceausescu placed signs along the highways. We saw many of these declaring, "Ceausescu is Popular" or "*Securitate* is *Pace.*" Needless to say, these stirred resentments.

23

Undercover

JEFF AND I TRIED our best to avoid being known behind the Iron Curtain in Christian or other circles. We maintained a low visibility, developing only trusted contacts for disbursement of mission funds, humanitarian supplies and literature. On occasion, Westerners who had briefly visited Eastern Europe to meet with high profile persecuted Christians came to our attention. Friends would ask, do you know so and so? Like satellites dispatched in the night, consigned to silence, we kept our distance.

Some pastors in our hometown made such trips. One was arrested, thrown out of Romania and arrived home in a blaze of glory. I worried the Christians who had arranged his itinerary might have suffered repercussions. Fortunately, there were many serious-minded pastors and lay ministers who recognized the precarious situation confronting the brethren in the East. They understood that to attract attention to themselves would put others at risk.

Door of Hope International zealously protected the persecuted and oppressed. Much of our success can be traced to the principles we learned in mission training, particularly from Paul Popov. He was a master on the subject of Eastern Europe and knew first-hand how to navigate there. As a young man, he and his sister Rhoda had smuggled their Uncle Ladin, who was imprisoned for his faith and later became a hunted fugitive, out of Bulgaria. Ladin Popov's book *The Fugitive* tells his story. When Ladin and Haralan began Evangelism to Communist Lands, now known as

Door of Hope International, Paul helped in every imaginable way and that included smuggling Bibles.

In the '80s two families of persecuted Soviet Pentecostals that Paul dubbed the *Embassy Seven*, ran past armed Soviet soldiers into the American Embassy, seeking protection and the right to emigrate. Despite the Kremlin's heated objections, the US Embassy in Moscow granted them asylum. Clutched tightly in theirs hands as they rushed past the guards to safety were the names and addresses of two US sponsors Door of Hope had provided.

Paul secretly entered the embassy and filmed an interview with them. He and his co-worker, Valerie, smuggled it out of the U.S.S.R. The filmed interviews were used to produce a one-hour television documentary, which was broadcast across America as, *Let My People Go.* It featured Efrem Zimbalist Jr. and Haralan Popov with the *Embassy Seven,* and presented the plight of the church in the U.S.S.R. at the time.

The Communists proclaimed their citizens had religious freedom. To substantiate this they paraded prominent Western politicians and pastors through showcased concourses and government-controlled churches. Paul and Valdemar Krause, a colleague who pastored a church in Germany, decided to disprove their lies. They drove to the Bulgarian border with five Bulgarian Bibles in a bag. When they declared the Bibles and offered to pay import taxes, the authorities beat them. They then took their pictures and declared them persona non grata. Paul returned to the States and published a report of the incident.

ONE SUMMER, K, S AND THEIR CHILDREN joined us at the base in Austria. Former missionaries to South America, K shared how their home church in the States had decided to gift their foreign missionaries with their used tea bags. K said, "They sent our family a barrelful of them as a gift. We were hurt and insulted. Their gift made us feel second rate."

Similarly, a dear friend and youth pastor in Bucharest shared an incident involving a group of Western pastors who had contacted him and asked for his help. He arranged for them to speak in various churches, translated and guided them around Romania for days, taking time out from his busy schedule. At the end of their tour when he dropped them at the airport, they thanked him and said they'd left him a gift in their hotel room to show their appreciation.

Stefan swung back by the hotel and found they'd left him a bag of their dirty underwear. He was hurt and humiliated. They had neglected to place themselves in his shoes, remembering Jesus' commandment to "Love thy neighbor as thy self," (Matt. 22:39).

Stories of such thoughtlessness were a small part of our experience. More prevalent were the accounts of God's miraculous loving kindness and care. One of my favorite demonstrations of God's grace occurred the summer K and his family came. The RVs were loaded, and K was to lead several teams into Eastern Europe. But two of the couriers scheduled to drive the campers had arrived without their financing intact. Everyone prayed and waited anxiously for a few days, hoping funds from the couriers' support base would come. It never did.

Jeff and I felt led to take up the slack. We wrote them a check for our last $1,000 and gave it to them. Every trip meant more Bibles to fill the hungry hearts of waiting Christians.

It was June, and the money was all we had left to live on until late October when we returned home and Jeff could earn more. As the teams left, we prayed for their safe return and for the protection of our precious friends in the East Bloc.

Jeff and I then walked to the post office to check our box. Mail was a high point in every missionary's life. Jeff drew out a letter from Bill Burnich, who handled our US bank statements in our absence. We read his note in awe at God's impeccable timing and marvelous provision. An unexplained $5,000 had been deposited in our Texas account. Bill had phoned the bank to report the error, but they showed a cleared deposit for the funds and insisted the money was ours. No one can beat God when it comes to giving. We gave everything we had, and God multiplied it fivefold.

Jeff and I have often been privileged to experience God's miracles in periods of need. Most of the years, as we passed in and out of borders, the one place they never searched was my purse. There were two exceptions, the first happened at a Romanian border on about our sixth year abroad.

It was illegal to carry Eastern European currencies in and out of those countries. On this particular trip as I approached the Romanian border, I had a large wad of their *lei* currency in my purse to aid Christians within. My purse had never been searched there before.

When our vehicle reached the border, guided by an inner sense, I asked directions to the restroom, stepped inside and locked the door. Swiftly, I removed the *lei* from my purse and wrapped it with some toilet paper I carried for personal use. I buried the wad in the middle of a waste-basket filled with horrid filthy trash, then strolled outside.

Minutes later, a custom's official demanded my purse. He searched it thoroughly. Some hours later, the inspection ended, and our visas were approved for entry. Before we drove off, I slipped inside the restroom and retrieved the *lei*, thanking God for the Holy Spirit's direction.

JEFF AND I DEPENDED on the Holy Spirit for discernment. This was especially true when meeting the mission's former connections. There was always the risk some had turned informer. One afternoon we set out to contact an elderly couple in Bulgaria whose names were on an old list from before the purge. For safety, we parked some distance away.

In their apartment, we met them, their children and grandchildren, assessing them by degrees. Jeff said, "We bring you greetings from Haralan and Paul Popov."

They recalled Haralan had officiated at their daughter's marriage. The grandmother served us hard chocolates with moldy green centers, which we dutifully ate.

I sensed the family members weren't as they appeared. After we left, I whispered as much to Jeff and he agreed. Before long, we realized they were following us. We continued walking but we strolled away from where we'd parked. Our license plates, also marked on our passport visas, would have made it easy to identify us. Thankfully, they only knew us as Phillip and Kathryn.

Eventually, we lost them and retrieved our car. Before they even followed us, the Lord had alerted us to be on guard. There was nothing specific we could point to that tipped us off. They had talked and acted friendly, but there was this inner warning telling us to be careful of what we said and did.

BENJAMIN COCAR USED TO EXCLAIM, "I can't understand, except by the miracle of God, how you two return year after year and are never caught." Without a doubt, God *made our feet as hind's feet*, (Psalm 18:33) in those days, seeing us swiftly and safely through the rock-strewn paths of Communist dictatorships, secret police and informers.

If it were possible, I would share the many practical methods God encouraged us to put into motion to ensure success. Still even today, though Russia is sometimes called our friend and former enemies have joined NATO, the mission's methods must be protected for we know not what the future holds.

The pace Jeff set probably contributed greatly to our success. The business of life in third world countries is slow moving and laborious, weighted down by the inefficiency and bureaucracy of Five-Year-Plans and Communist Manifestos. By the time the authorities were aware of an influx of Bibles or visits from the West, we had moved on to another country. If it had been left to me, I would have invariably set a milder pace, but it would have been nigh impossible to slow Jeff down. I followed happily in his wake, backaches and all!

In the West, Jeff and I compromised on autobahn driving. I suppressed any complaints about his speed of one hundred miles per hour, and he agreed not to go any faster. This worked well.

One autumn Paul asked me to drive the Volvo from Spittal to Stockholm for his use at an international board meeting. Afterward, we were also scheduled to drive several board members in the mission van to Helsinki and from there, catch the train to Russia.

I drove the Volvo in the drizzling rain, winding up and down mountains with Jeff impatiently following in the van. It was a beautiful drive. Yet on the German autobahn, in order to maintain a speed pleasing to Jeff, I was forced to constantly change into the fast lane to pass slower traffic. Cars were bearing down on me at what seemed like two hundred miles an hour. And if I stayed in the slow lane with the trucks, we moved at a mere sixty.

Near Munich, the vehicle in front of me was moving about one hundred miles an hour, much too slow for the daring motorcycle riders who surrounded and kicked the car with their boots. The frightened driver skidded across the autobahn almost causing a pile up. Afterward, I was even more hesitant to merge into the fast lanes.

Jeff signaled for us to pull over and explained that like it or not, I was going to have to drive faster, and I did. When I fell asleep that night, images of oncoming cars and trucks repeatedly jerked me awake.

The next morning in *Nürnberg*, feeling a bit sorry for his insistence the day before, Jeff took me on a brief tour of the city and ushered me into one of the more exclusive shops, buying me a lovely outfit before we continued on.

When we finally arrived in Stockholm, to show his appreciation, Paul booked us a room at the Sheraton instead of the usual youth hostel. It was a brief respite before our upcoming journey into the Soviet Union. I was happy to be there and enthusiastic about the days ahead.

24

The Fifth Wheel

IN ITS EARLY DAYS, the mission often worked with independent missionaries to deliver its stockpiles of Bibles. Some of them welcomed us warmly, while others were skeptical, considering us too naive and unskilled to succeed.

In the past, W had worked in Eastern Europe out of the Austrian base and now dropped by occasionally to check on us. His teams routinely ran RVs with loaded secret compartments into the Middle East.

Jeff confided to W our dream of building an RV to increase our present capacity, enabling DOHI couriers to carry thousands more Bibles on each trip.

W warned, "It takes seasoned skill to accomplish such a task," inferring we should leave such matters to veterans.

Helpful European acquaintances had pointed this out to us in numerous areas. For example, in Austria a home answering machine for the telephone is provided and installed by trained experts for $1,500. Amid dire warnings from friends about the difficulties we would encounter if we dared to do this on our own, we nevertheless bought a US model and set it up for less than $100.

One of the first phrases in Austria I learned to say when shopping was, "*Ich sehe mich nur um.*" Translated this means, "I'm just looking," and saying this afforded me the opportunity to make choices without undue interference. Austrian shop clerks were educated to recognize precisely what the customer needed.

In a society where citizens were taxed for using the airwaves on their radios, there was a procedure for most everything. Austrians could be quite fun-loving and adventurous, but independent-minded Americans were more used to cutting through red tape. Jeff and I were not exceptions. Back home in Texas, he drew plans to build a fifth wheel camper that could covertly carry either five thousand New Testaments or 1,100 extra-large full Bibles. This would double the mission's capacity for each trip. Paul supported us, but we needed the US board's approval to obtain the necessary funding.

One morning Paul phoned and said, "I presented the idea to the board, although Dad fought me pretty hard on this. So keep praying."

In time, Door of Hope International sent enough funds to launch the project. The contributions of friends in the Conroe area helped support the project as well.

A BSF friend, Bobbie Russell, contacted her dad, a former CIA agent with far-reaching contacts abroad. He ran a private-eye firm in the Midwest and offered us help in several crucial areas. On a visit to his daughter, he studied the fifth wheel plans Jeff had drawn and found no flaws. He had a lot of good things to say about them, which weighed well with Paul and the board. God in His infinite wisdom and mercy amazingly brought all this together.

At one point, we had contemplated smuggling Alex and Mimi Gitchev's two children out of Bulgaria. Bobbie's father kindly offered to help set this up with his former contacts. Thankfully, the children were ultimately able to depart through diplomatic channels.

When we visited their home in Monterey to confer on the translation of the *Bulgarian Open Bible Study Bible*, Mimi confided, "I could never forget you and Phillip. You were willing to risk your lives to bring us our children. I pray for you both every day."

Her words moved me. I'd never realized she knew Jeff and I were involved.

Like so many colleagues from then, we would always be Phillip and

Kathryn to Mimi. Former high-profile Bulgarian journalists, Alex and Mimi worked for Door of Hope International and later the US State Department until Alex passed away in 2006.

The fifth wheel plans were approved. Our neighbor Bill Burnich and volunteers, such as Norma, a California paralegal who stained the cabinets, worked with Jeff to build it in our backyard. It was an expensive project, frequently on the verge of halting due to financial difficulties. We spent hours on our knees discussing this with God. The Lord intervened again and again, allowing the construction to continue.

One bleak winter morning, there wasn't any money left. The work had been stopped for three days. I knelt and pleaded with God.

That afternoon Paul phoned, "Dad is flat out against this project. He says it's impossible to carry so many Bibles through Communist borders at once and too dangerous to even try."

My spirits sank as I cried inwardly, God, show us your plan.

Paul said, "You have one chance. Dad's flying into Houston tomorrow where he'll be speaking at several churches. Go to his hotel and talk to him. Try to convince him because I sure can't."

We agreed to make the attempt and considered Paul's call an answer to prayer. Once before when we were at a standstill, a widowed friend had handed Jeff $1,500, which he advised her against giving, due to her limited income, but she insisted.

On Saturday, Jeff and I drove into north Houston to Haralan's hotel, eager and anticipating God's intervention. Blunt and honest, Haralan didn't hesitate to declare he was against the project and proceeded to elaborate on why.

By then Jeff and I had been toiling in the mission fields of Eastern Europe for some years and understood the vehicles and borders in a way few did. We explained to Haralan why the fifth wheel was necessary and why we believed the plan would succeed. The situation was not unlike our approach to border crossings, in that we knew God was on our side. When we finished speaking, Haralan questioned us thoroughly, and in the end gave the project his blessing.

Paul phoned later. "I don't know how you did it. Dad is so far in your corner on this, he's being unreasonable."

"What do you mean? I thought you were for it."

He chuckled. "I am. Dad's making it difficult for all of us. He wants the board to send you the entire funds to complete the construction now."

My heart leapt with joy. "Fantastic. It's exactly what we prayed for. I don't understand the problem."

Paul sighed. "We can't fund it all at once without cutting elsewhere. DOHI has myriad responsibilities and can't just drop other ongoing projects or the support of pastors and missionaries in the field. These things take patience." He hesitated. "Maybe we can somehow enlarge the pie to give the couriers a bigger slice. Perhaps the mission can do an appeal. Let me get back with you. Meanwhile, keep praying."

Astonishingly the funds came through. There would be no delay. Our dream to have the fifth wheel ready and shipped in the spring to use for Bible deliveries became a distinct possibility, though a few more hurdles remained.

By March, the new RV was built and ready to be shipped, but the mission didn't have a truck powerful enough to pull it. Paul wanted us to buy a diesel truck, since the fuel cost less. We only had $7,000 to spend. In the early '80s, diesel pickups in good repair at such a price were almost nonexistent. Spring was nearly upon us. Jeff and I had been searching, with little results.

To show her support and encouragement Doris Edwards, the pastor's wife at First Baptist in Conroe, had asked me to speak at the ladies' monthly luncheons on several occasions. Haralan also spoke at their church, as it happened on his birthday. Pastor Edwards had the choir sing "Happy Birthday" as a surprise for Haralan. Typically, he felt it was a waste of the precious minutes he needed to explain the plight of persecuted Christians.

I greatly admired Doris. She was a wonderful Christian lady in every sense. After lunch, I stood behind the lectern and told them of our last season's work abroad and at home. I showed slides of the places we'd been, the people we'd met and the construction of the fifth wheel. I ended by asking them to pray for the Christians in Eastern Europe, our work and a truck to pull the fifth wheel.

Doris asked for specifics on the truck, such as the year, make, mileage, etc. and then led the women in prayer. That afternoon Jeff received a call from a car dealer in north Houston, and we purchased the truck from his lot for $6,700. Peter Wannemacher, a friend and flight attendant, drove it to port in North Carolina, and we picked it up in Rotterdam. How miraculous is our God!

The advent of the fifth wheel greatly increased the number of Bibles delivered, though not just anyone could drive it. Jeff and I couldn't. Due to our extended exposure, Paul considered us too great a risk. The two of us continued to coordinate the couriers' trips and usually traveled by car to these rendezvous, pulling one of the mission's pop-up campers to sleep in. This saved on hotel bills.

Before the fifth wheel slipped into port, a profile search for the best courier-driver combinations had already begun. I fondly recall visits with LaJewel, sitting in her living room, discussing and praying about the upcoming candidates and deliveries. We avoided specifics that could endanger courier operations. She kept a group of BSF leaders and friends updated, which gave us tremendous spiritual support.

Despite all efforts, the Midwest couple chosen to drive the fifth wheel were challenging. On the surface, D and A seemed perfect. He was an experienced commercial driver; she was a sweet, competent working wife, or so it appeared during their interviews and training. Both had excellent references from their employers, church, family and friends. They received the appropriate instruction and preparation, as did all mission couriers.

Their RV was loaded, and they were sent off to Romania with much prayer. Jeff and I planned to rendezvous with them in the Sighisoara campground. When they didn't arrive the first evening or the next, we fought against a sickening fear that the worst had happened, while peppering heaven with prayers they would make it. Two days later, they arrived mid-afternoon.

A was nearly hysterical. She wanted to ditch the RV, take a train to the base, pick up her bags and fly home. I sat on a bench in the camp, trying to calm her. She confessed to an aspirin dependency due to a nervous condition. "I was terrified they would find the Bibles and arrest us," she said.

A sinking feeling in the pit of my stomach, I prayed. Why, Lord? How did we end up here with them? We had tried so carefully to screen applicants. Now everything was at risk. The truck was stamped on their entry visas. The authorities would only allow them to leave the country in the fifth wheel. The law prohibited anyone else to drive it across the border.

It was loaded with Bibles and any nuance of change spelled trouble. The vehicles and literature could be confiscated—Jeff and I arrested or banned—the base discovered.

Lord, we need your help more than ever. Work in A's heart. Protect us and Your Word. Such were our silent prayers.

We realized A and D might have already let something slip at the border and unwittingly led the militia directly to us. Jeff and I exchanged worried glances. They could be watching us surreptitiously. As scenarios raced through my mind, I tried to discover from A where they'd been for the last thirty-six hours and what had happened with customs. Meanwhile, Jeff talked with D.

A said, "From the moment we entered Romania, the authorities acted suspicious."

Had her nervousness tipped them off? I listened to the neurotic woman before me, mourning the loss of the confident woman I'd interviewed earlier.

She continued. "Romania held us at the border for a day and a half, searching the RV. They didn't find any of the secret compartments. Guards ripped open the bags of milk powder and boxes of laundry soap you put in the cabinets for Christians and accused us of carrying cocaine."

"It's not so unusual," I said. "Once I had some purple candles, which they suspected were rockets."

We had tried to make appropriate choices through prayerful and careful screening. Sometimes we failed. Not everyone is called to this work. In our weakness, it was more important than ever to rely on God, believing, "all things work together for the good of those who love God . . ." (Rom. 8:28).

D and A had been forewarned to expect adversity and taught how to react in various crisis situations. The last thing we wanted was to have unprepared volunteers falling apart when faced with routine Communist aggression and intimidation tactics.

LaJewel and Buni used to say, "Christians are like tea bags, you never know what kind they are until you put them in hot water." I guess that goes for all of us.

The good news was the fifth wheel had withstood one of the toughest searches it would ever encounter. Still, we were concerned about the state of A's nerves and the possibility they might have led the militia to us.

Her husband D took the situation more in stride and helped us to eventually calm A. The next step was to ensure no one was tailing us. So for two days we drove around, acting like tourists on vacation. Meanwhile we prayed, battling an oppressive and persistent fear. Jeff and I watched the car mirrors for signs we were being followed and noted the faces of those around us on every street we walked.

Finally, we made the plunge, unloaded the Bibles and sent D and A swiftly out of the country in the fifth wheel. Everyone managed to soothe A enough to handle the trip out. Needless to say, they did not return as couriers the next year. Some people are so direct they can't handle covert operations. We were grateful they were able to finish the mission. They even talked of returning but we neglected to extend another invitation and they never inquired about the omission.

The fifth wheel went on to become instrumental in our work, making it possible to deliver thousands and thousands more Bibles behind the Iron Curtain each year. Its advent also encouraged DOHI's European offices and individual donors to provide funds for similar projects. Daniel Voumard and his wonderful wife Janine negotiated two such vehicles through DOHI Belgium. There were so many who helped in myriad ways—we'll always be grateful. The many couriers who sacrificed their vacations and savings, annually returning to smuggle Bibles and deliver aid, were the backbone of God's work through us.

25

Ted and Shirley

ONE SUMMER THE HOLY SPIRIT warned Jeff, the fifth wheel should not be used. The couple scheduled to drive it accused him of being fearful and pessimistic. A mood of dissent arose at the Austrian base. To lean on the Holy Spirit for direction was essential in every aspect of our lives for without God we were lost. It would have been easy to appease others and send the RV out despite the check in our spirits, yet how much riskier in the long run it would be to ignore God's prompting.

Courier trips continued while the fifth wheel rested in the garage. The next season it was on the road again. Through the years, it sailed across borders with only a few minor casualties. Small mishaps often caused major delays, like when Judy and Bill took the fifth wheel on an autobahn test drive from Spittal to Salzburg. A Yugoslav van, thrown off guard by a semi changing lanes, halted in the middle of the freeway. The semi stopped to keep from hitting it and the blue Ford diesel pulling the fifth wheel slammed into the back of the tractor-trailer. No one was hurt, but the truck's hood was crumpled, and Ford auto parts weren't available locally. We had to wait for Bill Burnich in Texas to ship a new hood from the US, resulting in about a month's delay.

Austrian customs weren't the easiest to clear. Without careful paperwork, the tax levied could exceed the item imported.

One fateful day we were all caught unaware. After years of successful trips, we became a little careless, and fate aligned with time and chance to demand restitution. When it happened, Ted and Shirley were driving the fifth wheel to Romania. Like many of our earlier couriers, by then, they were seasoned pros and able to lead teams safely in and out of Eastern Europe on their own. There were some rules we never broke, such as divulging where the addresses of the Christian brethren were hidden. To this day, I have kept the secret. Only those who had been proven trustworthy were permitted to handle these addresses and learn the secrets of hiding them. Just before the teams headed out, members met in our office for briefings. Lastly, we met with the team captains in private to review contacts and give them the addresses.

On this occasion, rather excited, Ted said, "Shirley and I've come up with a new method to hide addresses." He pulled a stick of spearmint chewing gum from a pack in his front pocket and showed us the writing in ink on it. "What do you think?" he asked, with an eager look.

We stared at the gum, covered with tiny ballpoint penned addresses.

"Interesting," Jeff said, intrigued.

Ted continued. "I could swallow the gum before anyone could get to it."

"I like it," Jeff said.

"I don't know," I said uneasily. "We should put them where we normally do. It's always worked and there's no question of them being safe."

"What could go wrong?" Jeff asked.

As the three of them quizzed me and we hashed this out, there must have been some discussion regarding the necessity of developing new methods and branching out. These were valid points. A certain amount of daring was requisite to smuggling Bibles. It wouldn't have been the first occasion when I opted for the traditional path because it was familiar and secure.

Ted's idea looked easy. And I had to agree, it would take about three seconds to get the gum from his pocket into his mouth. I still didn't like it. I could feel the general consensus; I was being too cautious. With a reluctant shrug, I relented.

As usual, prior to the team's departure, everyone gathered in the kitchen and we prayed before sending them off.

Days later, when the phone call came, we were stunned and stricken. Shirley and Ted had been caught. For forty-eight hours, the Communist authorities had intimidated, mocked and cross-examined them. Then abruptly, they were released, turned back from the border, miles from any town with nothing but the clothes they wore. Ted and Shirley walked to Hungary where they hitched a ride to the nearest city, which was about fifty miles away. From there, they rang the base.

Jeff and I rendezvoused with them at a hotel in Hungary. A haggard expression on his face, Ted said, "I've never seen anything quite like it. When we pulled up to the Romanian border, the guards were strip-searching everyone."

Shirley chimed in, "Ted tried his best to undo the wrapper and swallow the gum with the addresses. But the guards tore it from his hands before it could reach his mouth."

Ted said, "When they saw the addresses, it was over. The officials called for their supervisor and ordered drills and saws on the spot. We've never prayed so hard."

The four of us shared a look of knowledge teeming with commiseration. Our hearts were one when it came to Bible deliveries. The enemy had pounded us with a setback. I thought of the prayers and months of labor that had gone into the construction of the fifth wheel and I wanted to weep. I managed to smile. "What happened next?"

Ted frowned. "Armed militia surrounded us. Then we were separated."

Indignant, Shirley said, "We were strip-searched, then threatened and interrogated for two days and nights. The officials asked what we knew about some smugglers called Phillip and Kathryn Jefferson."

Jeff and I exchanged charged glances. "What did you tell them?"

"Absolutely nothing," Ted said in a satisfied voice.

Shirley added, "A few hours before we arrived, customs had torn apart someone else's RV and found Bibles. The Romanians were on a rampage to uncover more."

Bloodthirsty for new finds, customs had begun systematically strip-searching both Easterners and Westerners as they entered the border area. Jeff and I had never known this to happen before. Still, it took them hours of drilling, sawing and tearing apart the fifth wheel before they found the first Bibles. After that, there was no stopping them.

Even in the midst of this disaster, God sprinkled His blessings. Because Romania was poor and needed money, the authorities confiscated the fifth wheel, then offered to sell the destroyed RV back to Shirley and Ted for $5,000. Its initial cost was much higher, and we were determined to get it back. What a blessing that Ted, who was a banker, donated the $5,000 to recover it!

Later, Jeff phoned our friend Bill in Texas who had helped build the fifth wheel and related what had happened. "Any chance you can take some time off work and fly over here to help repair the damages?"

"Man, I'd love to help. I don't know if I can swing it though. Let me talk it over with Diane and call you back."

The Lord opened the door for Bill to come and handle the repairs gratis, and he did a great job. Soon the fifth wheel was back on the road. Though it could no longer be used in Romania, it remained useful in other countries.

Ceausescu was a maverick and infamous for his lack of cooperation with his Warsaw Pact neighbors. His determined stubbornness had ensured there were no Soviet soldiers there. This led us to reason Romania wouldn't easily share its intel with other nations.

The first test trip into Bulgaria was fraught with risk but proved fruitful, and the fifth wheel entered the country safely. The fifth wheel served the mission faithfully through the years until the fall of the Berlin Wall and the end of Ceausescu's tyrannical reign. DOHI then donated it to several churches in Romania where it is still used as a mobile Christian coffee shop. When it stops, locals are invited inside for coffee, discussion, literature and videos.

Scripture tells us that without a vision, God's people will perish. We all need dreams to strive for in our daily lives. When the Lord authors those dreams He sees them through to fruition just as He did with our dream to build a larger RV to carry more Bibles to those in need. How great is our God!

26

Friends from Texas

WE NEVER TIRED of the border guards' expressions of wonder whenever the pop-up camper was opened for inspection. The small flat trailer unfolded into a six-foot high orange canvas tent, with a pumpkin corduroy queen bed on one side and a metal floor on the opposite side. Though simpler than most American models, to the East Europeans it was magical. The most hardened officials gaped in amazement as the trailer morphed into a tent.

DOHI had a fleet of these little pop-ups we had purchased second-hand in Copenhagen for $135 each. They were also used by our Friendship Evangelism teams. Jeff and I preferred them to many of the hotels, which were often bugged and closely observed by the secret police. Hotels were a likely place to pick up a tail.

Benjamin once shared an amusing story of several Romanian pastors attending a convention. They searched their room for bugs and found what they imagined to be a hidden microphone. The pastors cut the electrical cord, sending the chandelier in the dining room below crashing down.

Occasionally, we stayed at hotels to take baths, wash our clothes in the tub and enjoy warm meals. One time in Timisoara, Romania, before checking in, we asked if there was hot water. "Certainly," said the man behind the reception desk. When we reached our room there was no hot water. I called downstairs and was assured by the same clerk, "*Mâine.*"

"I won't be here tomorrow," I said exasperated.

"There's nothing I can do," he said impatiently and hung up.

This scenario was par for the course.

EARLY IN THE SPRING OF '85, our friends, Ronnie, his wife Linda, and Larry accompanied us on a three-week journey through Czechoslovakia, Poland, Romania, Bulgaria and Yugoslavia. Jeff and I had arrived at the Austrian base before the courier season started so we could show the Texas group around Eastern Europe and introduce them to fellow Christians. Once the teams began arriving, we always seemed to be needed in three places simultaneously.

Larry had volunteered for a brief stint with DOHI while his wife and kids attended a youth camp in the US. For the past sixteen years they had lived in Belize, where Larry trained native teachers and pastors for church and seminary work. This was his first vacation in fourteen years.

Interestingly, when asked what inspired him to become a missionary, he said, "I once heard a man, Haralan Popov, speak and it changed my life." When his family read Haralan's book *Tortured For His Faith*, the children asked their parents not to buy them any Christmas gifts. "We'd rather you bought presents for Christian kids in Communist countries."

Carol and Larry did just that. I've never been so moved. These children, who lived frugally in the jungle with their family, had so little, yet they were willing to give abundantly to others.

It was an honor to have Larry with us and we had such fun. The Diamond was loaded with Russian New Testaments and Czechoslovakian children's literature.

At the Czech border, we sat around the RV table, laughing, joking and playing canasta, while the guards probed the vehicle inside and out. If we were caught, our entire group could serve a mandatory prison term. British missionary David Hathaway had been sentenced to four years in a Czech prison. Fortunately, he was freed early. We were aware that any overt anxiety on our part would be viewed as suspicious.

Linda's generous smile exuded warmth, inviting others to join in the

123

fun as she laid down a card and said, "Your turn." Gifted with a voice that spread a charm of its own, she hummed a bit, doing her part to distract the guards.

Though it was risky having Jeff and me aboard, the searches weren't as comprehensive in Czechoslovakia and we weren't well known at this particular entry point.

Despite outward appearances, everyone was alert and praying. When the inspection was finished and our visas stamped, we hid our relief, inwardly praising God in gratitude until it was safe to let go.

Later, we delivered the children's material to the mission's Prague contacts, rewarded by the delighted smiles on their faces as they thanked us again and again.

I was usually more disorganized during the first and last trips of the year. Initially, I struggled to gear up for the season, and by the final jaunt, overwhelmed and weary, I invariably let something slide. We journeyed on to Poland and sure enough, I had forgotten our towels. Linens were only sold every other month. Jeff shared his extra T-shirt, and we took turns drying with it.

Our group visited some construction sites where youth camps were being built. We gave Russian New Testaments to several of the churches the mission supported there. The plan was for Polish Sunday School classes to hand-address parcels and mail the New Testaments as part of an outreach to the Soviet Union. We anticipated few problems with these Scriptures, passing through Polish and Soviet inspections undetected.

A highlight of the visit was an evening spent in the home of a pastor's son. He and his wife invited a few couples from their congregation. After dinner we discussed the distribution of the Russian New Testaments. It soon became apparent our Polish friends saw this as an opportunity to earn money for their building projects. They asked DOHI to pay them $1 for every testament they mailed, plus postage. The situation was delicate. The mission cheerfully supported their building projects and various endeavors. Still to pay for what any Christian should be willing to do was too much.

Though poor, Poland fared better than most of their East European neighbors. Czechoslovakia was the exception, and also did well, due to heavy industrial development evidenced by the black smog hovering over its cities and roads, which had Europe complaining of acid rain.

The impetus behind Poland's economic boost was Western aid. Some said the Soviets systematically drained the country of this aid and paid the Polish Communist government to cooperate. Some experts believed the U.S.S.R. devised schemes to obtain Western Polish aid as a means to help finance their own military efforts.

Poland's economy was by no means robust. Though there was food and money for building and restoration, prosperity among the Warsaw Pact nations could in no way be compared to the affluence of the West.

Larry, who had gladly sacrificed years of his life ministering to the natives in Belize, had been listening quietly. He began to give his testimony to our Polish friends, who were deeply moved. The rest of us chimed in and by the time we left they were grateful and excited at the opportunity to help those less fortunate than themselves. It surprised them to learn how blessed their circumstances were, compared to such places as Romania, both in matters of economy and, to a lesser degree, religious persecution.

From Poland, we drove to the base and switched to the passenger van, then set off for Romania and Bulgaria to prearrange with contacts for the season's upcoming deliveries. We left Ronnie and Linda with Pastor Veselin and his wife Magda in Plovdiv, Bulgaria. They organized a secret retreat in the mountains where Ronnie taught a large group of pastors, while Linda ministered to their wives.

Meanwhile, Larry, Jeff and I headed back to the base, stopping over-night in Yugoslavia at a hotel in Nis. Larry chose to save money and sleep in the van. There was nothing I wanted more than a hot shower. I hopped in, only to find the drain didn't work. The rapidly rising overflow of water made bathing impossible. Jeff phoned the reception desk and requested another room, but the clerk insisted on sending a plumber upstairs instead.

This sounds simple enough in the telling, but it was complicated and filled with nuances of paranoia and suspicion. The hotel, one of the best in the area, retained the aura of a third world nightclub and routinely practiced intimidation techniques. We didn't want to see a plumber, but to refuse was not an option.

At about 2:00 a.m. the militia arrived at our door in uniform, toting a gun. He checked us out as well as our belongings. As for the shower, he shined his flashlight in its direction and shrugged to indicate there was nothing to be done. Security (what a misnomer) had little to offer in the way of plumbing repairs.

We washed up in the sink. Then I tried to sleep amid the prevailing sense that our space had been invaded—that we were of special interest—and maybe they knew more about us than they should. Sometimes within a fifty-mile radius of the border, countries cooperated to the detriment of our work. And we were within that radius.

Thankfully, the three of us drove off early the next morning without mishap. A journey across Yugoslavia was always an experience. The traffic on the roads put one's life at risk. Our base was about a sixteen-hour drive from Nis, most of it a meager two-lane highway void of shoulder lanes.

Every summer thousands of immigrant Turks who worked in Europe traveled this road to Turkey to see family. Europeans driving to Romania, Bulgaria, Greece, Macedonia, Albania or Turkey also took this route. Add to this the East Europeans on vacation and the slow-moving military trucks clogging the roads.

The result was life-threatening chaos, comprised of two packed lanes of traffic, one going east and the other west. Traffic moved at about thirty miles an hour unless one passed the slower vehicles ahead. To travel from Nis to Spittal in sixteen hours, passing was a must. And 70 percent of the drivers were similarly compelled. Hence, we drove constantly, either pulling into the next lane of oncoming traffic, praying as hard as we ever did at any border, or having cars face us down in our lane.

I'll never forget one particular trip in the pickup camper. Bear in mind the traffic doesn't wane through the night. About midnight, Jeff pulled into the oncoming lane to pass a large convoy truck and the camper stalled. A steady stream of autos surged directly at us, leaving no place to go as we stalled alongside the truck we were striving to pass. Miraculously, the two lanes of traffic adjusted, and Jeff steered the camper until it engaged, squeezing back in behind the truck.

There was a small stretch of autobahn, two lanes in each direction near Belgrade. In Europe, slower drivers kept to the right, leaving the left lane to those moving at higher speeds. As we journeyed from Nis, Larry drove in the left lane within this section of autobahn. Jeff and I tried to convince him to stay right when not passing. But Larry, used to Belize where the natives are more laid back, tended to tune us out.

Finally, two Turks in a Mercedes pulled alongside the van, yelling at Larry. He looked across and saw one of them waving a foot-long curved blade at him. Stunned, Larry swiftly moved into the right lane for slower traffic and stayed there for the rest of the trip. He had learned the predators of Yugoslavia were dissimilar beasts to those in the distant jungles of Belize.

27

A Sense of Humor

IMAGES LINGER, FUGACIOUS MEMORIES of scenes unique, because they brought a brief respite in their unexpectedness: Like the morning we were one umbrella short at the Hotel Ambassador in Bucharest. Jeff and I had stepped from the elevator into the rose-marbled foyer. It was one of those dreary, rainy days, as much a part of Romania as the fellows hanging out in the lobby waiting to tail anyone they found suspicious.

We approached the reception desk, and two of the men closed in to see what we wanted. The one with the secret police leaned his elbow on the counter and studied us. He appeared to be in his sixties but could have been half as old. If there were a market for aging formulas, the Communists would have been wealthy. They had the formula down tight. The man was of medium build but appeared strong in a tough sort of way. He had gray hair, a craggy face marked by cynicism, and frown lines pushed the corners of his mouth down. They all have this telling look, these men assigned to shadow others, and out of necessity, most of them carry umbrellas.

We gazed past him to the clerk. Five or six umbrellas rested against the wall behind him. Jeff asked in German, a common language many Europeans spoke, "Have you got an umbrella we could borrow or rent?"

He eyed us with stony mistrust. "*Nein.*"

Jeff gestured toward the pouring rain outside. Everyone turned to stare out at the dismal day.

I thought of the grocery bags, filled with milk powder, canned meats and laundry soap, in the van. I'd added generous helpings of chocolate and chewing gum to each sack for the children. We had several to deliver and the weather would make a mess of the paper sacks.

The follower seemed to reflect gloomily on the hassle of shadowing people in the rain, probably wishing foreigners like us would stay home.

Jeff's teasing grin invited the men to share in the humor of the situation. "Come on, there's no hotel parking and our car is a few blocks down the street."

The clerk's set expression made it clear he would not be relenting.

Jeff sighed and discreetly pulled out a five-dollar bill. "We're going to get soaked. I know you have one back there. I'll give you this five for the use of it, and we'll return it tonight."

The clerk shook his head.

Jeff turned to the follower and offered him the money for his personal umbrella, but he refused as well.

I wasn't surprised; he appeared the more formidable of the two. He unbent enough to explain, "You walk in some shop and forget it, then I have no umbrella. And no place to buy another. It's not easy here like in America."

"I'll tell you what," Jeff said. "I'm going to perform a little magic." He waved his closed black umbrella dramatically and lifted it above his head. "Watch, very carefully. You're extremely fortunate. I don't show my secrets to just anybody. Notice, I'm using only one hand." In a pronounced, elegant maneuver, Jeff pressed the button on the handle. "Poof!" Flaps of spoked black fabric spread in a circle over his head.

The two men watched in wide-eyed amazement.

Jeff chuckled. "Let me use yours. If I don't bring it back, I'll give you mine."

A gleam of avarice lit the follower's eyes, and he handed his umbrella to Jeff.

Satisfied, we left to meet our contacts and deliver the aid we'd brought. In the evening, we returned his umbrella.

ON YET ANOTHER VISIT to the Hotel Ambassador in Bucharest, black marketeers milled across the street, on the prowl for foreigners they could persuade to make a deal. They traded for jeans, food, coffee, aspirin, the clothes we wore or cash. It didn't matter. As long as it was Western, there was a market for it in Romania.

We were walking to our car when a Gypsy sidled up to Jeff. "Change, Mister, change. I give you primo rate. Forty *lei* for every dollar." The official value was six to one.

I shook my head and walked faster, warning Jeff against banking with strangers on the street. "There are Christians you can trade with who need dollars to pay for milk or a doctor's visit for a sick child."

He hesitated and the Gypsy moved closer, a skilled handler dangling unbelievable offers to bait the trap. Jeff said, "The extra cash would help our friends."

I whispered of dire consequences, but Jeff was hooked. "Go back to the room and wait for me," he said.

He left with the Gypsy, in clear view of the hotel and the watchers within. "You could have at least chosen a nice secluded spot away from prying eyes," I muttered to his retreating back. What if this was a set-up?

He and the handler strode down the street and turned the corner.

Later, Jeff told me the Gypsy flashed a large wad and separated out 1,600 *lei*, passing it to Jeff who recounted the bills before giving them back.

Jeff kept his gaze trained on the *lei* as he drew out his $40.

Suddenly, the Gypsy screamed, "Run. Police." In a flash, he grabbed Jeff's hand and covered it with his own, sliding the *lei* into Jeff's palm and closing it fist-like over the money. Simultaneously, he seized the dollars from Jeff's other hand and fled.

Jeff slipped the cash into his pocket and sauntered back to our room. "I told you there wouldn't be any problem. Here, I'll give you some of my *lei*."

He pulled the wad from his pocket and stared aghast at the stack of neatly cut newspaper, sandwiched deceptively between two Romanian bills.

This also happened to Paul Popov, who out of curiosity embarked on an experiment to see how the marketers switched the money for newspaper, when the three of us were in Bulgaria. Afterward Jeff and Paul both wore rueful expressions, still unable to figure out how the Gypsies had tricked them.

———————————

IN YET ANOTHER HUMOROUS INCIDENT, Jeff and I were in Prague working our way through a roster of Christian contacts Paul had given us. We were nearing the end of the trip, and phoned one of the last names on the list.

Jeff spoke with the man briefly and managed to get us invited to his apartment, situated in one of those Communist gray concrete complexes. His place was stylish, with new furnishings, TV and stereo. An amiable handsome blond, he struck us as more sophisticated than the average persecuted Christian. We visited for a bit, randomly feeling our way. The conversation went something like this:

"So do you know Maury?" he asked.

"No." Jeff shifted uncomfortably, not daring to mention anyone we knew in case the man was an informer.

"American, aren't you?" he asked.

"Yes."

"Did Double P send you?"

We exchanged quick glances, wondering who Double P could be.

When in doubt it sometimes helped to answer a question with one of our own. "Do you know many Americans?" I asked.

"Only Double P."

We were back where we'd started. Our host looked as uneasy as we felt, though he covered it well. "I'm not sure if we do," I said. "How long have you known him?"

He hesitated a moment, sizing us up in a nonchalant manner. "We met last June. He said he might be sending friends who would need help."

"What exactly can you do for us?" Jeff asked.

"Can you tell me what Double P stands for?"

Neither of us had a clue, then all of a sudden it dawned on us. We said, softly in unison, "Paul Popov?"

The man smiled. We soon learned, though he wasn't a Christian, he'd helped Paul contact some who were in prison. He was also a safe source for changing money. Naturally, just as Paul had, we witnessed to him. I'd like to think our visit bore fruit.

IN A SIMILAR VEIN, Grace, Jeff and I were in Plovdiv, Bulgaria, late one evening, looking for a certain contact. It was in one of those large, depressing East European buildings with people stacked inside like kipper snacks in oblong cans.

We inadvertently knocked on the wrong door and were inside seated in the living room, visiting with the young man who lived there, before we realized our mistake. Soon there wasn't a doubt in my mind that God had led us there specifically.

The man was a practicing Communist who had been taught God was a myth created for the weak. Moreover, he was in the middle of a personal spiritual revolution. His wife had recently died, and in his grief, he searched for new answers. God heard his silent keening, saw his anguished vulnerability, and responded to the broken man within. Secretly, he began to pray and read the Bible he'd found hidden among his wife's belongings. Finally, he prayed, "Please Lord, send someone to show me how to be a Christian."

Teary-eyed, he shared the horror of his wife's death. Hot water was such a rare commodity, it was common to heat it with cup-size portable heaters used to make coffee. His wife ran her bath water, immersing the element and setting it afterward on the side of the tub. She slipped into the steamy mist and the element she'd forgotten to unplug fell in, electrocuting her.

Grace translated as we talked of God's miraculous forgiveness and His redemptive plan of salvation, encouraging the young man with Scripture. Grace led him in the sinner's prayer, and we rejoiced as he accepted Christ as his risen Savior. We told him about Veselin and Magda's church a few blocks from his home and urged him to attend and learn more of Christ.

Later, we shared his story and address with Veselin and asked him to visit the young man who went on to become a valued member of their congregation. Grace, Jeff and I felt blessed. Our work in Eastern Europe seldom allowed us the luxury of sharing Christ with nonbelievers. Our mission was to bring the necessary tools, Bibles and humanitarian aid so national pastors and lay leaders who understood the culture and spoke the language could minister more effectively. God in His infinite goodness had lifted our hearts.

28

John from Bucharest

WE FIRST MET John Cochuba in Bucharest at his abode, with his children and petite wife beaming a welcome. They lived not far from the area where Ceausescu was ordering entire neighborhoods to be systematically destroyed to clear the path for his palace of culture, which was to house the government, the *Securitate,* his family residence and more. It has since been renamed the Palace of Parliament.

John was middle-aged, his physique short and compact. He had rich brown hair and a perceptive gaze that peered through dark horn-rimmed glasses with warm sincerity. His boyish face held a firm resolve, hinting at strength one could depend on.

As young missionaries we were enthralled to see history dramatized as we never dreamed possible. I still remember sitting at the dining room table, listening to Paul and John speak in German, directing shipments of contraband Bibles across Romania and into the Soviet Union. One always felt the gentle power of the Holy Spirit in John's steady gaze and flow of words.

When he stood, long aluminum crutches cupped elbows and hands, supporting his legs and allowing him to swing his limbs forward as he walked. Yet, his quiet personality was such, the braces quickly receded into the background as instruments that facilitated his movements, both physically and spiritually. Because John was crippled and viewed as weak by the Communists, his whereabouts were of little interest to authorities.

Thus, he journeyed throughout the country for the most part unhindered, wise enough to take advantage of this factor.

We felt privileged to work with this man who, behind the scenes, was legendary for the innovative and daring plans, upon which more than one mission depended for success. For years, Jeff and I had heard whispers of Scriptures smuggled routinely into the Soviet Union by Romanian dump truck drivers. At John's, we learned the true story behind this miraculous drama, and were thrilled beyond measure to be given active roles.

Though John was the organizer, clearly God was his director. Paul arranged with John for Door of Hope International to smuggle thousands of Russian Bibles into Romania to certain contacts who would then drive them into the U.S.S.R. Many Romanians resented the Soviets for plundering and subjugating their country. This made it even more critical for the Bibles to reach the right individuals there.

Eventually, we met John on our own, freeing Paul to work in other areas as we took on more responsibility. One day Jeff and I drove with John from his home to the Bucharest train station. Inside, women, old before their time with creased faces and coarse gray hair wrapped in scarves, mopped the floors. The buckets of gasoline-reeking cleaner they swabbed onto the cobblestones left a trail of white-waxy streaks. The odor covered the stench of bathrooms hosed down, amid the shuffling crowds of hungry and needy people.

Businessmen, dressed in fashions evocative of the '40s and '50s, mingled in the crowded station with the Gypsies and peasants, united in their desire to avoid the armed militia and plain-clothes agents stationed throughout. This scene, and like settings, will always be etched in my mind in shades of black and gray. The women wore faded washed-thin flowered dresses that buttoned down the front. The colors long since muted, the large-flowered prints they favored sucked dry of any remembrances of things past. That which was once white had yellowed and grayed, leaving dinginess and soot in its place.

We booked couchettes in a second-class sleeper car with six persons per room. The berths were narrow and hard, and we slept little as the train rolled toward the northern edge of Romania, bordering the U.S.S.R. At about 5:00 a.m. we gathered our few belongings and debarked in the town of Suceava. To the west the rolling green foothills merged into mountains, dotted with the steeples of Orthodox churches. Nearby, the village women drew their water from a community well.

Two smiling pig farmers met us at the station in an old Lada that had seen better days. They drove us to their home, where we were ushered into a small farmhouse with dirt floors. The plump hostess kissed and hugged us, and others shook our hands with joy. Guiltily, I yearned for a cup of coffee, an item practically nonexistent in Romania.

Our hostess fried fresh farm eggs in lard and served them dripping with fat. Despite an aversion to lard and anything greasy, particularly on an empty stomach, I ate with seeming delight. Tired and dirty, I smiled at the gray-haired woman who eagerly watched us eat, clearly desiring to please us.

Afterward, they led us to the living room to await John's contacts. Colorful tapestry rugs decorated the stucco walls, helping to seal out winter's chill and summer's heat. Jeff and I sat on a worn sofa, which was a reflection of the room at large, shabby but comfortable and clean. John settled into an old wooden chair across from us. At night, the room passed for a bedroom.

As we talked, John studied us intently and read from the Apostle Paul's writings in the book of Romans. "'With the heart man believeth unto righteousness; and with the mouth confession is made unto salvation . . . For whomsoever shall call upon the name of the Lord shall be saved,'" (10: 1–13). He shifted in his chair.

Jeff and I glanced at each other expectantly, wondering where he was leading.

John continued, "Please, don't misunderstand. To bring Bibles is good, but to preach God's Word is better." He drew his Bible out again and read.

"'How then shall they call on Him in whom they have not believed? And how shall they believe in Him of whom they have not heard? And how shall they hear without a preacher?'" (10:14, 15).

Jeff looked thoughtful. "You're saying the Bibles we deliver help individuals, whereas a single sermon can reach hundreds or maybe thousands for Christ."

"That's right," John said. "What you and I do for my country is the second most important thing, because for every hundred Bibles we bring, a preacher or evangelist is born."

John's words made quite an impression, and their significance still resonates with me. It gave me a warm sense of satisfaction to know that when I provided others with Bibles, God was working beyond the present, raising up young men and women to follow Him in the ministry and to preach the gospel.

I couldn't help but think of other verses in the same chapter of Romans, because their meaning fit so precisely with what John had been saying. "How beautiful are the feet of them that preach the gospel of peace, and bring glad tidings of good things! . . . faith cometh by hearing, and hearing cometh by the word of God," (10:15, 17).

Later that morning, we met with Romanian farmers and truck drivers, the true heroes of this theater, and arranged for them to smuggle Russian New Testaments across the border. These brave Christians risked their lives and freedom, concealing DOHI shipments of Scriptures in the middle of the dump truck loads of gravel they drove into the Soviet Union. These believers and their wives hazarded all to deliver God's Word to a country that had ravaged theirs. I still recall their endearing smiles and daring zeal.

Christ said, "Greater love hath no man than this, that a man lay down his life for his friends," (John 15:13). He also promised, "whosoever shall lose his life for My sake shall find it," (Matt. 16:25). When the Communists first invaded Romania, they dismantled life as those who labored under their harsh regimes had known it. Then as they moved out, they placed

Ceausescu in power, leaving an uneducated dictator who strove to rob the people of their freedom, religion, individuality, children, farms, houses and ultimately the lives of friends and family.

Yet, these Christian farmers gave back good for evil. I am awed to have known and worked among them, and to serve the God whom they serve, in whose strength our weaknesses are made perfect, (2 Cor. 12:9).

29

Jealousy

JEALOUSY IGNITED a tumultuous sensation in my gut. Despite a closeness with my husband, which friends exclaimed about, I was literally eaten up with the green-eyed monster. We were on a speaking tour in France with a week's itinerary before us. Elisabeth, DOHI's French director, was our guide, translator and chauffeur to the various cities and churches. On the road, she directed most of her comments to Jeff, who seemed to expand under her undivided attention. Mile after mile, I listened as they talked and talked and talked. They were both on the mission's international board and had much to discuss. Jeff tried to include me in their conversations, but his efforts failed. As if passing my days in this manner weren't enough, Jeff wanted us to spend our first free evening with Elisabeth.

Furious, I paced back and forth in the kitchen of the small apartment the church in Grenoble had provided for our brief stay. How could he be so blind? From the kitchen window I could see her seated at an outdoor café down the street. "No," I said. "I'm not going and if you do, I'm leaving."

"You're being entirely unreasonable," Jeff accused.

Guilt assailed me. How could we be fighting like this? Tomorrow we would be doing radio interviews and addressing one of the largest evangelical congregations in France. I was reminded of the Bible verse, "Beloved, think it not strange concerning the fiery trial which is to try you, as though some strange thing happened unto you," (I Peter 4:12). I'd never been so bewildered, hurt and trapped. I looked at Jeff. "Can't you try to understand? She rarely even speaks to me."

"She doesn't ignore you intentionally. You're the only one who notices. It's natural she'd want my opinions on certain projects."

Finally, we compromised. If we met Elisabeth, Jeff promised to talk to me equally, whether she did or not. I knew the rest of the week was going to be difficult. I had just finished an especially trying six months working behind the Iron Curtain. I felt drained, as if I had nothing left to say or offer anyone. Elisabeth appeared fresh, vivacious and excited. In my heart, I cried, Lord, please let Jeff understand how I feel.

Two nights later, we visited a church in Dijon. Rather than Elisabeth, the church preferred we use their translator. He was a handsome Frenchman who ignored Jeff and addressed every word he said to me. What a perfect illustration God had sent us!

Jeff and I spoke to the congregation, then the man sat between us and interpreted the rest of the service, whispering in my ear as if Jeff did not exist. Afterward, the man attached himself to me during the fellowship.

Later, when we were alone, Jeff asked, "Don't you think the church translator acted kind of strange?"

"How do you mean?"

"Well, he translated everything for you as if I weren't even there. It just seemed odd."

Relief surged through me. "I thought so too. He acted like Elisabeth has been acting the entire trip."

I saw the light dawn in his eyes and along with it the concern and understanding I was so used to. Thank you, Lord, I whispered as we hugged. Together we could face just about anything.

Sometime later at home in Texas, I asked a few close friends to pray with me about the next year's tour in France. As it happened, the following fall,

Jeff and I were double booked to speak at twenty-three meetings in two different countries during the same week and had to split up. He spoke in Belgium and I presented the ministry with Elisabeth in France. Elisabeth and I grew close on that trip and have since enjoyed many delightful visits together. I believe, in her mind as she watched me work, Jeff and I became equals. God's answers to our prayers couldn't have been better!

30

Buni and Marianna

AT OUR CONROE HOME, the phone on my desk rang and I picked up the receiver.

A heavily accented Romanian voice said, "Hello. This is. . . ."

He paused and I raced to say, "Buni Cocar." As if I could ever forget him. I smiled as memories of midnight rendezvous delivering Bibles while our hearts raced tugged me into the past. "Buni, how are you, and Marianna and the children?"

"Three kids in university. We're struggling but making it." He added, "I'm not sure what to call you anymore, Kathy or Jeana."

"Call me whichever you like. I answer to both." For years the Cocars knew us as Phillip and Kathryn, two American missionaries who often showed up in Romania with Bibles and relief items.

When the mission learned that Buni and his wife spent two days every week washing the family's clothes in the bathtub, DOHI bought them a washing machine at the dollar shop in Bucharest. Jeff, Buni and I pushed, shoved and dragged it from the street to their flat, while furtively looking for any signs we were followed. This was done in broad daylight across an area with thousands of flats in gray concrete buildings. His apartment was several flights up.

Buni often helped us as well with practical details. When our car had a bad tire, he knew a trusted mechanic to fix it. Or if the auto stations ran out of gasoline or were out of electricity, making it impossible to pump the gas, he might know a friend who had some to sell so we could continue our journey.

"How are you and Phillip?" he asked. We hadn't spoken in months, yet the past bound us irrevocably. He continued, "I received a postcard saying you'd moved."

"Yes, after twenty-three years, we finally built a new home."

"You're still in Conroe though and working for Door of Hope International. I hear you're an important editor now."

"I'm only managing editor. Paul's editor-in-chief," I said, referring to DOHI's president. "How about you? Are you still pastoring?" When Ceausescu's regime forced the Cocar's from Romania, Buni chose to settle in Chicago where there were thirty thousand unchurched Romanians.

"I'm pastoring two churches, but I'm thinking of retiring soon. There are plenty of younger men to take my place." Buni was also director of the Immigration Service's Department of Mental Health in Chicago. He sounded humble and awestruck, as if he couldn't quite believe how greatly his life had changed. After a life of persecution by authorities in Romania, his abilities and qualities were now appreciated and rewarded, so different from his life before.

Buni used to joke that Romanian walls were half concrete and half microphones. He had more reason than most to know the ins and outs of Ceausescu's *securitate*. One summer Jeff and I drove most of the night to rescue Buni's family in the aftermath of what must have been one of the bleakest periods of his life. The secret police had bulldozed his church's building, destroying it. The authorities had then collected his mother from the hospital where she was dying from cancer. They took her, Buni and his pregnant wife Marianna and left them outside the sprawling city limits of Bucharest on the side of the road. They were told to leave. Buni and Marianna were not allowed to take their three young children or say goodbye. The situation was tragic, yet their faith never wavered. God stood with them through the darkest moments of persecution. Jeff and I were in awe of the tremendous anointing of God on their lives.

The incident happened in the '80s when the Romanian economy was in shambles and the people were in despair. Milk was a black market item, and few dared to buck the system. Buni's brother Benjamin pastored a church in Medias. His Uncle Mircu and Cousin Daniel were pastors as well and his Cousin Rodica was head secretary at the Baptist Union in Bucharest. She had a beautiful voice trained for opera and sang in many of the churches. They were great friends and part of DOHI's distribution line to their country and much persecuted for their faith. Their zeal for Christ won converts at a rate that alarmed the Communists. That summer we had stopped at Benjamin's home first and learned of Buni's family's plight. Benjamin called around to find out where they were, and we drove halfway across Romania to pick them up.

When Jeff and I arrived, Buni's mother had already died and Marianna had miscarried. She looked extremely ill, her face yellow. We drove them back to Bucharest to find their children. Later, Buni took us to see the rubble that was once his church.

Eventually, the Communists forced both Buni's and Benjamin's families to leave the country. The morning of their departure, fifteen hundred Christians came to see them off, risking arrest. They sang softly as their dear friends left on the plane; these bright lights in their dark lives departed for a new life in America.

Benjamin moved his family to Detroit, accepting a pastorship in a town where there were sixty thousand unchurched Romanians. He went on to add an American doctorate in theology to his Romanian one and taught at Michigan's Baptist Seminary. Buni added a Master's in psychology to his theology degree. He also became Billy Graham's translator for annual Romanian conferences and traveled frequently, ministering abroad.

Some years later after the collapse of the Iron Curtain as we talked, catching up on each other's lives, Buni said, "I read one of your magazines recently. You're doing a lot of work in Kosovo and the Balkans." We spoke of this for a bit and then he admitted, "After everything we've been through, I feel as if I'm getting old and staid, not doing enough."

Both of us knew he was doing plenty and I told him so but quite understood his feelings. I sometimes felt the same, though mostly Jeff and I were glad to sit in our living room in our favorite wing back chairs, reading or talking quietly, just the two of us. We'd experienced God's anointing in an extraordinary way—His presence and protection tangible in the midst of dramatic upheaval. That period was hard to surpass, for challenge. Yet God is everywhere and no less present now than then. Desperate need and challenges do, however, heighten one's perceptions.

Buni asked, "Isn't there a revolution in South America or someplace where you could use me?" The question was facetious, and it held an underlying yearning. "How about in Venezuela or Argentina?" he asked, citing areas where his command of Latin languages would be useful.

After we hung up the phone, Buni's comments stayed with me for weeks, a subtle and familiar fragrance rehearsing Godly dramas of victory. Maybe someday soon there would be another revolution to join. Maybe the East Bloc would continue to erect new barriers to religious freedom. Reports from there revealed a troubling number of cracks in the present administration's tolerance of Christians. For the sake of our many friends there, though, I hoped communism was on the decline.

31

Weary

EVENTUALLY, I REACHED a point where the intense pressure of the work overwhelmed me, affecting my ability to cope. I had confronted fear and jealousy, but now I found myself in a battle to hold on to my sanity. I clung to God's Word, saturating my soul with its strength and comfort. "For our light affliction which is but for a moment, worketh for us a far more exceeding and eternal weight of glory; while we look not at the things which are seen, but at the things which are not seen: for the things which are seen are temporal; but the things which are not seen are eternal," (2 Cor. 4:16, 17).

In despair, I cried out to God—I didn't want to be weary in well doing. Yet I listened to the plight of persecuted Christians with a new, numb impartiality, weighing one person's needs against the next. Jeff counseled this was natural, the mind's way of protecting us, like a scab covering a wound. We could only absorb so much before experiencing overload.

When Paul arrived at the base in Austria that summer, he noticed I was on edge. He told Jeff to rent us an apartment, and the mission would pick up the tab. For the past five years, a partial wall had separated the office from our bedroom. And with the ongoing teams and activities, we were seldom alone. In Spittal, there were 981 people on waiting lists for apartments. Still, the Lord provided us a place of our own, though it involved four moves and a lot of expense before we were settled.

As Jeff and I assumed more duties in East and West Europe, our couriers were taking on more responsibilities too. Also, the two of us were not traveling together as often. We seemed to be needed simultaneously in different places. I grew accustomed to sleeping alone and would awaken startled if Jeff was there beside me, fearing an intruder. He often led Western pastors on tours through Bulgaria, Romania and the U.S.S.R., while I ensured the work at the base continued running smoothly.

In a sense, I felt as if I were losing my identity, the present obscuring and submerging everything kindred. Most of the activities we enjoyed prior to our involvement with DOHI had gradually dropped from our lives until it seemed the ministry consumed us. Yet there was more need everywhere we turned.

Once, in Moscow, I recall, we'd returned from meeting with underground contacts at about 3:00 a.m. The two of us stood whispering in the dark hotel hallway. To economize, Jeff was sharing a room with a Canadian pastor, and I was with Ruth, a Russian Canadian friend and our translator. Jeff and I were both bone weary, and I had a bad cold as well.

"Get me your shirt for tomorrow and I'll iron it," I said, prolonging the moment, because I missed being with him.

He touched my hair lightly. "I've already done it."

A bittersweet sense of loss squeezed my heart. When had he begun to care for himself without my help? I didn't even like to iron. Yet, I missed performing the familiar small tasks even those I'd never been fond of, such as ironing Jeff's shirts and packing for him.

Each year became busier than the last. Jeff was elected international VP at DOHI. As we trekked home to the States annually, the growing distance between my old life and my new life seemed to expand into an invisible barrier, separating me from my past. Friends chatted about Little League, football scores, the arts or other events, all a universe away from the gray Communist world and the people's burning need for Bibles. A sense of loneliness haunted me.

In Texas, we would walk into the grocery store and, like most Europeans, be overwhelmed by the choices. Instinctively, when people spoke English, our minds translated it into German so we could understand. Jeff and I had grown so used to trouble shooting covert operations, we couldn't enter a room without subconsciously probing for defects. Life had become deadly serious. A mistake could cost us so much.

Everything came to a head one fall in the late '80s when we arrived home after being abroad. I attended my beloved BSF class where so many dear ones upheld us. After opening hymns and prayer, we divided into small groups to discuss what we'd studied in the week. Our young leader struggled to get the discourse moving. Following a long silence, I started to answer one of the questions.

She interrupted. "Why don't we give someone else a chance to answer."

Everyone tensed. I understood she wanted some of the shy women in the class to talk. I smiled, but my hurt feelings amplified my aloneness. Our leader tried her best to get the group to respond. I sympathized and hoped no one had picked up on my inner turmoil, which was more about what was going on within me than what was happening there.

Finally, she said, "Jeana, I think you've been quiet long enough."

The last question answered, we filed back into the sanctuary for LaJewel's lecture. I sat in the pew, battling tears and depression, amid hundreds of BSFers, many of whom were devoted supporters. Why couldn't I feel God's presence and the warm cocoon of their caring? What was wrong with me?

Afraid I would embarrass myself and burst into tears in front of everyone, I slipped out of the church, climbed into my car and drove away. Unable to see through my falling tears, I pulled off the road and bawled. "God, why do I feel so bleak? Please, there must be a reason." There were no answers for me then, not any I could perceive. I struggled to compose myself enough to drive home.

Later in the afternoon, God visited me in an extraordinary manner. The room didn't shake and there were no visions, but His words spoke into the dryness of my soul, bringing knowledge and healing. "The foxes have holes and the birds have nests but the Son of man hath not where to lay His head," (Matt. 8:20 KJV). His voice seemed to say, "And so it is for My followers."

Jeff and I had never quite fit into the tight circle of missionaries in Europe. Many viewed us as part-time, because we worked for DOHI stateside as well. We also belonged to a US mission, another stigma, because Americans could never understand Europe as well as Europeans did.

This was merely background, another grain of grating sand. Leadership was a solitary proposition. Paul had asked us, with rare exceptions, to maintain a distance from other missions to the East Bloc, which meant declining most offers of assistance and comradery. There were hotel ministries for the sole benefit of Bible couriers. Yet we never stopped at these places.

Paul feared these lodgings would be easy for Communist spies to infiltrate. Once they identified the vehicles and missionaries coming and going, it would be a snap to arrest them later with their illegal cargoes. Paul's strategy worked. I don't know of another ministry that enjoyed DOHI's high rate of success, and our isolation was one of the reasons.

At home, it seemed as if our friends' lives were moving on without us. The couriers and staff we worked with were spread across the United States and Europe. Jeff and I were weary from the long hours and the miles traveled, and the ever-present spiritual battles as we defiantly entered territories where Satan claimed dominion.

The Lord brought all these thoughts to mind, and I began to perceive the whys of displacement and loneliness, the grinding of years passing. I could bear most anything if I could just understand what was happening to me.

As I knelt in my bedroom, praying, God gave me the answers I sought. He spoke to my heart. "Loneliness is a bridge to a closer relationship with Me."

Could I use this loneliness as a bridge to grow closer to Christ? The answer was a lifeline, which brought immediate comfort, though the struggle remained.

During this period, Jeff was wonderful. He never criticized me for being weak. He accepted I was going through a difficult time and engaged in spiritual warfare. He knew I wasn't usually prone to tears but had a fairly optimistic nature. 1 Pet. 3:7 took on new meaning, "Likewise, ye husbands . . . give honor unto the wife as the weaker vessel. . . ." In my weakness, Jeff encouraged me with his faith and loving-kindness.

We don't have to be missionaries to feel under attack. I often think of those who have lost children, endured illnesses or had spouses walk out on them. There are many roads to sorrow and displacement, but God is always there waiting to help us around the bend if we'll let Him. LaJewel used to say, "Don't waste your suffering when it comes. Make sure it counts for something."

Our sorrow lasted a short season and, in its wake, came our most productive and satisfying years.

32

Chernobyl Disaster

SHOPPING FOR THE BASE was an international affair. Wherever Jeff and I traveled, we hunted for bargains. Mission appliances were purchased locally, much of the team's food in Italy, pots and pans, music and books in Hungary, art and glassware in the former Czechoslovakia, pop-up campers in Denmark, file cabinets in Sweden and trucks and RVs in the United States. We remained on the alert for any means to stretch the courier budget.

One of DOHI's best finds was the San Lucesio, a Catholic hotel for missionaries of all faiths in Amsterdam. Its rate was half that of most hotels, and the location was a convenient ten-minute trolley ride from downtown. The sisters served a generous Dutch breakfast in a room overlooking the garden terrace. For lunch and dinner, guests were on their own, and in the evenings, some gathered in the communal living room to watch the news or a movie and visit with other missionaries passing through. We felt blessed to be there, particularly on the many occasions we were required to wait for one of the mission vehicles to clear port customs or needed to sleep off some jet lag before resuming the journey to Austria.

Those Amsterdam days were informal and low-key. We delighted in walking down the cobbled streets, the smell of the sea and its breeze at our backs. An afternoon spent at the Rijks or Van Gogh museums and we were in heaven.

The spring of 1986 stands out as unique because during the Reagan administration the US bombed Libya, putting Americans abroad on edge. Jeff and I flew from Houston on April 16, the day after the bombing, and landed in Amsterdam jet lagged. The two of us seldom unwound enough to sleep on planes no matter how tired we were.

We left our luggage in lockers at Schiphol Airport and caught a train to Rotterdam, which held Europe's largest port. I kept drifting asleep and awakening with a start, fearing we'd missed our stop. Once there, we rode a tram to the dock and walked to the port warehouse. The area bustled with nearby freighters unloading cargoes offshore. A pleasant clerk processed our paperwork and soon we drove off in the 1984 blue Ford diesel pickup. DOHI had shipped the vehicle across the ocean to pull the fifth wheel.

Jeff and I retrieved our bags from Schiphol and headed to the San Lucesio. Jeff parked the conspicuous pickup with its Texas plates in front of the hotel where we could keep an eye on it. It was twice the size of any other car and with the media warning of terrorist threats to Americans abroad, we were uneasy.

Up in our room, we showered and slept for a while, then walked to a nearby Greek restaurant we liked. Invariably, Jeff preferred the quiet off the beaten path places one always worried might go out of business, because they remained for the most part undiscovered. The candlelit café, the lamb and feta salad and the congenial back and forth chitchat with the owner as we dined, created a soothing balm of sorts. The next day we would indulge in the hot and spicy Indonesian food as popular with the Dutch as Indian curry was to the English, and for much the same reason—the influx of former colonists.

Back at the San Lucesio, Jeff and I stopped by the community room to catch the news before going to bed. We conversed in German with the room's sole occupant as the news program flashed pictures of the bombing in Libya, with the three of us inserting occasional comments on the incident.

I glanced from the TV screen to our companion's black hair and eyes and darkened complexion, thinking he might be from the Middle East. Curious, I asked, "What mission are you with?"

He hesitated, and when he spoke, his German had a Middle Eastern ring to it. "I'm not a missionary but on my way to England for business reasons." At our questioning looks, he continued. "A contact from my school days arranged my stay here."

Jeff shifted in the large overstuffed chair. "Where are you from?"

On the TV, the newscaster was saying Qadhafi's son was reported to have been killed in the bombing of his father's presidential palace. There was a pause while the three of us digested this.

Jeff looked across at the man, as if he might have missed his answer. "Where did you say you were from?"

He threw us a rueful look. "Libya." He failed to elaborate, and we didn't inquire any further.

Immediately, in our minds, we tried to retrace our comments. Did he know we were Americans? Surely, it was obvious. Our unease returned and, as soon as we politely could, we said good night and went back to our room.

"It's probably nothing," Jeff said, stretching out on one of the twin beds, his feet hanging off the end.

I lay down on the other one and stared up at the ceiling thoughtfully. "It's too weird to think a terrorist might be at the San Lucesio of all places. His visit is likely perfectly legitimate."

We both agreed. Still, our training kicked in with what-ifs . . . And there we were with the pickup parked out front. After some discussion, we decided on a plan we were more at ease with.

We slept a few hours, then left under cover of darkness, wanting to get the truck to the base ASAP, where it would draw less attention. Thankfully, all went well.

———————

LITTLE DID WE REALIZE then, in a short time, the Chernobyl disaster would send Europe into a panic. Jeff and I were in Spittal, setting up for the summer's work that same spring of 1986. We awoke on the morning of April 26 to shocking news. At 1:23 a.m., the Chernobyl Nuclear Power Plant, in a deadly experiment, had allowed power levels to drop too low in the fourth reactor. It overheated and caused a core meltdown, resulting in two explosions blasting the top off the reactor. Sweden was the first to report the incident.

Worry of cancer and radiation sickness were rampant during the next two weeks as clouds of deadly radioactive materials were flung into the atmosphere across Europe. The Austrian government asked people to remain in their homes to avoid contamination from the high radiation levels, which could be tracked into homes. We were told if we must go outside to take off our shoes before we came back inside. Rain only added to the trouble, washing the toxins deeper into the soil.

Officials warned that fresh food supplies, including vegetables, meats and dairy products, were contaminated and not to be eaten. Gardens had to be uprooted. As far away as Wales, fourteen years later, more than four-hundred farms remained condemned due to the nuclear fallout from the incident. The news reported Ukrainians in Chernobyl were exposed to levels of radioactivity many times higher than that of the Hiroshima bomb. Europe was exposed too. The wind blew clouds of the radioactive material northwest.

According to the BBC, in Chernobyl thirty-one were killed immediately and in the aftermath, another fifteen thousand relief workers who strove to contain the disaster died. An additional fifty thousand relief workers became invalids. Children aged fifteen or younger were especially suscepti-ble to thyroid cancer, which increased at an alarming rate in the Ukraine.

The World Nuclear Organization's report updated in April 2020, states that only two died at the time of the accident due to the explosion and twenty-eight died in the aftermath due to radiation exposure. Their report cites the "'United Nations Scientific Committee on the Effects of Atomic Radiation has concluded that, apart from some 6,500 thyroid cancers (resulting in 15 fatalities) there is no evidence of a major public health impact attributable to radiation exposure 20 years after the accident." Some organizations have alleged that the U.N. has white-washed the effects of Chernobyl in order to uphold the safety of Nuclear power.

At the time, Jeff and I were deeply concerned, not only for ourselves but also for the Christians we worked with in the area. DOHI had a number of contacts in Kiev, which was only eighty miles from Chernobyl. We had even been arrested in the Kiev region when we accidentally took the wrong road and ran into a convoy of rocket launchers.

I thought of the pastors, their wives, children, congregations and entire cities exposed to the toxic radiation, and all I could do was get down on my knees and pray. I have to admit there were some prayers offered up for our own safety and protection. Again, it was a lonely feeling, being there in the middle of such a catastrophe with home, family and friends thankfully far removed.

There came a day when life had to resume for three hundred and fifty thousand displaced Ukrainians as well as ourselves. The vegetables had to be blessed and eaten, shoes wiped as best as one could to cut down on the transfer of radiation. Thankfully, we never experienced any ill effects from the nuclear fallout. The Chernobyl exclusion area remains uninhabited decades later, although some (estimates vary from one hundred to one thousand people) have returned to the city, mostly the elderly and those who had nowhere else to go. In subsequent trips to Kiev, the city appeared to have recovered, although deformities from the radiation and cancer effects seemed more apparent among its citizens.

Most of those we worked with in the Ukraine were fine, though I have read heartbreaking accounts from those who lived in Chernobyl when the reactor blew. A letter to DOHI from a scientist, ill with cancer and unable to care for his family, pleading for help and prayer, comes to mind. The mission has tried to give assistance in such cases, especially to the children.

In Spittal, Pastor Alexander Ferrari's Swedish Alliance Mission held its first summer camp in 2002 for Chernobyl children with cancer. Another camp was scheduled for 2003, but sadly, our dear friend, Pastor Alexander Ferrari, a dedicated missionary and church planter passed away. Eventually, his wife Erna retired to the apartments DOHI had refurbished for courier use.

33

Austria

WITHOUT THE AID of Alexander and Erna Ferrari, it would have been difficult to maintain our cover in Spittal. A tall man with a huge smile and a heart as soft and sweet as honeycomb, Alex reminded me of a giant teddy bear. He creatively hinted to the town's residents, I was a wealthy writer, and Jeff, the owner of a successful travel business. I wrote some articles for DOHI and was working on a novel. Jeff probably felt like the leader of a Christian tour company, albeit one uniquely promoting travel to places most tourists avoided. And we were rich in the Lord.

Though Alex and Erna seldom knew particulars, they prayed fervently for DOHI operations and did everything in their power to assist. Whenever I needed a prescription for a Christian behind the Iron Curtain who had a threatening heart condition or other illness, Alex knew the right person to ensure the believers received the necessary medicine. In extreme cases, he even arranged for specialists to travel to the East Bloc.

His wife helped in countless ways as well. We were introduced to them as Jeana and Jeff during our first spring in Austria. Later, when we became couriers, Alex had trouble remembering our code names. He would pause in the middle of a church service, groping for the right name. He'd finally gesture my way. "You know who I mean, the one with the face like the *Mona Lisa.*"

My long dark hair and round face, in a country of blue-eyed blondes, led him to make the comparison. In reality, even younger and slimmer as I was then, there was little similarity. Despite Alex's occasional fumbles, our pseudo identities at the base remained intact. In a small city the size of Spittal, there were myriad reasons why it was virtually impossible for us to go unnoticed.

Those we came in contact with were often curious. Typically, each spring, everyone from the grocery checker to the teller at the bank would exclaim, *"Ach-so! Sie sind hier wieder. Wie lange bleiben Sie dieses mal?"* ("Aha! You are here again. How long do you stay this time?")

A smile hid my wariness. "As long as we can. This is our favorite place to visit. It's so beautiful." Truly God had gifted us with a charming base to work from.

"Ja! Ja!" they'd respond with a proud grin, their questions forgotten.

Or some might say, *"Sie kommt immer hier. Warum?"* ("You always come here. Why?")

And my reply again would be similar. *"Es ist so schön hier im Spittal. Es ist ganz wunderbar."* ("It is so beautiful here in Spittal. It is quite wonderful.")

Apparently, we were the only Americans living among them. Most of the oddities locals observed in our situation, they attributed to our nationality. For instance, I might be seen in the Volvo on Tuesday, and the Citroën, the Volkswagen or the Toyota on Friday. And then the following week, one might notice me leaving town in any number of RVs. This might prompt the question, *"Wieviel Autos haben Sie?"* ("How many autos do you have?")

With a shrug I'd respond, *"Es ist egal,"* meaning, "It doesn't matter."

My friend Anita said, "The Austrians have a saying, *'Die reiche Tante kommt aus America mit viele Geschenken.'*" ("The rich aunt comes from America with many presents.") This stereotype of the rich American bringing gifts worked to DOHI's advantage.

On the mission's behalf, Jeff and I spent thousands of dollars a month running the base. This fostered an illusion of wealth. There were even larger amounts of cash flowing in and out of mission accounts (all in Jeff's and my name, since technically the base didn't exist). These included bank transfers from DOHI offices in Europe and from as far away as South Africa, Australia, the United States and Canada.

Many of the money transfers were designated for specific projects in the East Bloc, and it was our job to deliver either the goods or the money. For example, if South Africa decided to contribute a PA system for a Soviet church, it might be more cost effective for us to buy and deliver it. Also, translators and editors had to be paid and salaries were sometimes funneled through missionary trips. Plus, there were large groups of couriers dropping in for extended stays, spending generously and promoting the notion of affluence.

Strict financial accounting was always maintained. Every item purchased was recorded and beside it, a description, the amount, project, department and country code entered. Monthly statements were sent to DOHI/USA and receipts filed for reference. Our personal finances were kept separate.

A good cover in Spittal was critical to maintain the anonymity of both couriers and vehicles. By law, in Austria, a stay longer than thirty days required an application be made for residency and any vehicles said applicant owned registered at the time. Because the mission's entourage of missionaries and autos traveled frequently in and out of the country, the base squeaked by on this requirement. In fact, the question never arose, thanks to Alex's intervention. We received the blessings of local authorities, which he passed on, enabling us to keep a low profile.

The European custom of daily shopping offered us a break from the base. In the summer as fifty thousand German and English tourists poured into Spittal, parking became difficult. Residents left their cars at home. The five-minute walk to town was faster than trying to park.

I would cut though the *Hallenbade's* lot around the corner from the base to walk to the post office to pick up the mail. Since it was so close, if there was time, I might stop by the Hotel Ertl where Herr Ober, the head waiter, would lead me to a table on the terrace. He wore his fitted green wool Kärnten jacket like a uniform. His short sandy hair swept back from a smiling, yet prim, oval face, Herr Ober's hazel eyes glinted commands to passing waiters and welcome to his customers. *"Grüß Gott. Ein schön Tag, nicht war."*

"An absolutely gorgeous day," I returned, relaxing on the oblong terrace encircled with ornate wrought iron, awash in hanging baskets and planters of pink and red geraniums. I could see the train station and Goldeck Mountain, looming purple and majestic in the near distance.

"Möchten Sie ein Koffee und vielleicht ein Strudel?" he would ask. ("Do you want a coffee and perhaps a strudel?")

"Ja, danke." I hoarded those moments alone; part of me has always craved some solitude. I scribbled notes for my first novel, *St. Abient Run*, and drew my protagonist Susan's character, on napkins there on the terrace, sipping coffee. Jeff and I occasionally enjoyed dinner at the Ertl, watching the sun set over the mountains or if it was cold we'd eat inside. Herr Ober always had a smile and a special place for us regardless of the crowds.

Several streets away, the park occupied a large square block downtown. Sidewalks crisscrossed the grounds. Seasonal flowers, shrubs and trees dotted the landscape. Grandmothers, garbed in traditional Kärnten dresses, their gray hair twisted into buns, ambled alongside teenagers in contemporary slacks and shirts—a delightful mix of old and new.

Children frolicked on jungle-gyms, swings and merry-go-rounds. Chess enthusiasts played on a huge stone game board, moving waist-high kings, queens and pawns. The park ended at the fountain in front of *Schloss Porcia*, a fifteenth century Italian castle that abutted the main street.

I enjoyed sitting on the park benches, watching as people hurried to the stores in preparation for lunch, their most important meal. On weekdays, businesses shut down from twelve to two. At noon sharp the town whistle blew, storekeepers locked-up and everyone rushed home. On Saturday at noon, it blew as well, and the town closed until Monday morning at eight. Often, a holiday before or after caught us unaware, and there would be no bread or milk.

The butcher, grocer, stationery, fine china and other shops lined the main street. I might visit the bookstore to see if there were any new novels in English. Jeff and I found reading German tedious, as most of our efforts had been directed toward gaining conversational skills as rapidly as possible.

Early on, we'd enrolled in a series of fast-track language classes at Houston's Rice University. Later, we took various night classes and arranged for private tutors both at home and in Austria. We also invested in Berlitz language tapes. These classes included an enormous amount of grammar with plenty of reading and writing, though the emphasis was on speaking.

Nearby department stores, such as Quelle and The Forum were ideal for household bargains. One day at The Forum, I was browsing through the discount glasses and spotted boxes of German *Zwiesel* Crystal. This was the last place I expected to find fine crystal for five dollars, even with the dollar's high value.

I turned to the salesclerk. "Are these really for sale at this price?"

"*Ja*. The buyer ordered them, but they weren't selling. Too pricey for our customers. So we marked them down."

Unable to believe my good fortune, I scooted around the corner to the fine china shop and found the same glasses priced at the equivalent of thirty-five dollars each. I zoomed back to The Forum and bought quite a few. Jeff and I have enjoyed these beautiful crystal glasses for years.

We also gave them as hostess gifts with three in a box, which boosted our image as rich Americans, though I had not considered this until I saw one hostess's reaction.

It's amazing how, whenever I thought we'd sacrificed so much, the Lord pointed out those whose actions went beyond what I'd ever considered. Or He might unexpectedly remove a prop I'd begun to cling to. He also provided nice surprises to lift our spirits. What a blessed adventure we experienced, serving God and discovering what He had in store for us next.

34

Rush to the U.S.S.R.

DETAILS OF OUR TREKS to the U.S.S.R. have blurred through the passage of years, however, it would be almost impossible to forget the occasion when we were arrested in the Ukraine. Such journeys were planned well in advance. Visas had to be obtained, courier flights booked, funds arranged, contacts in the East Bloc alerted, literature stockpiled at the base and vehicles designated.

Soviet visas were without a doubt the most frustrating to acquire. Detailed itineraries had to be submitted, listing each night's resting place and the roads to be traveled. Invariably, the Soviet Intourist's draconian bureau delayed approval, making it, indeed, quite a feat for us to arrive by the designated day. Should one fail to arrive on time, the visa expired, and the process had to be restarted from the beginning.

In July, six of us had gathered in the Austrian base office to discuss the upcoming trip. Worried, I said to Jeff, "We haven't heard a word on our Soviet visas, though we applied months in advance."

"There's not much we can do about it," Jeff said.

I sighed. "I was hoping we could take our time and spend several days in Romania, instead of racing through to the USSR."

"What route will we be traveling?" asked David, a recent ORU marketing graduate who also spoke Russian.

Jeff explained, "We'll divide into two teams. Both will approach the U.S.S.R. via Romania, driving across Moldavia, then swinging up through Ukraine and to Kiev. Eventually, we'll all exit at Lvov into Poland." Our travel companions included Phil, a Texas businessman, Tanya, a California secretary, Sonya, a concert cello player, David and ourselves.

Finally, the visas were approved. The Intourist agent warned us, "You have two days to reach the Soviet border before these expire."

Jeff, Phil and Sonya left for Romania in the VW Golf, pulling a pop-up camper. Another couple departed in the Diamond, which was loaded with Romanian Bibles. They were to rendezvous with Jeff's team there.

Meanwhile David and Tanya, who were to be our Russian language translators, and I headed to Vienna in the Toyota station wagon to pick up the group's visas. This was their fledgling trip. Consequently, as I drove and negotiated the autobahn, the streets of Vienna and the Soviet embassy, they saw me as a seasoned traveler. As the trip progressed, however, I felt less and less in control, despite a bold front. Still that afternoon, our visas in hand, we headed east.

Around midnight we took lodging in a home in southern Hungary that offered rooms for rent. David chivalrously carried in our luggage, setting a pattern for the nights to come, which I'm sure grew burdensome. Imagine the full-size suitcases of two women who had packed enough for weeks.

In the morning, we hit the road early, with two more Communist borders to pass through before we could meet the others in Romania. Passage through Hungary went off without a glitch. At the Romanian border, we navigated past hundreds of autos in line waiting and inched into the relatively short line for Western vehicles. When our turn came, the search was intense but thankfully took less than four hours.

In the afternoon, we met Jeff and his crew at a crowded campground in Oradea. Their tents rested beneath the shade of sprawling oaks, a long folding table set up with chairs in front. We sat and visited.

I turned to Jeff, anxious to hear the details of his trip there. "How long did it take you to get through the Romanian border?"

He grimaced. "Eight hours. They went through everything with a fine-tooth comb. It's a miracle they didn't find the material in the pop-up."

"I hope you at least passed up the East Europeans and went straight to the Western line?" Jeff was too nice sometimes. I lacked the patience for long border waits. Jeff felt guilty at passing everyone up, but I was willing to do whatever it took within reason to speed up the process. That included walking to the front of the line to find out what was holding us up, requesting cars to move if necessary to let us through, and even prodding the attending guards to get started.

No matter how far back in line we stayed, they were going to eventually move us into the Western line. So why not get there quickly? I had lots of practice on how to do this and still come off sounding like the most naïve tourist around.

I took a moment to study Jeff's face. "Did you get any sleep?"

"About three hours. I'm not too tired. I hung back a bit in line, then realized if we were going to meet the Diamond to get the Bibles, distribute them and make it to the Soviet border on time, I had to move forward." He squeezed my hand. "Though we didn't get all the Bibles delivered. How about your trip down? Did the Toy do okay?"

"Great." I filled him in on the details, and he brought me up to date on the Bibles he'd given to Romanian believers. Jeff and I were pleased with the teams. Phil was older than the rest of us, but he had an easy-going manner and an agile sense of humor. Tanya had a sporty look and was eager to pitch in where needed. Sonya was a pretty, soft-spoken, blonde with a fiancé back home.

On another trip, perhaps even in another year, Jeff and I spent days with her at an inn in the backwoods of Hungary when the automobile we were driving in broke down. A call for help dispatched a courier from the Austrian base with the necessary parts. Meanwhile, Sonya shared her stash of classic books, which we devoured. Intelligent and perceptive, she was delightful to work with wherever we traveled.

Soon the others joined us, and the conversation became general. The women put together sandwiches and everyone ate. The soft melody of a violin concerto drifted across from the next tent.

David caught my eye. "One of your favorite symphonies, isn't it?"

I nodded.

David had a wide smile and a natural Southern charm. His black hair, blue eyes and tanned strength had attracted the interest of several females at the base. He remained courteous and friendly but reserved, which discouraged their interest. One of the young ladies complained he kept his relationships shallow. With a hunted look, David said, "I like shallow. What's wrong with that?" Far from shallow, David was bright and a great help.

The schedule was too pushed to allow for our staying the night in Oradea. After dinner, we loaded up and hit the road. And what a terrible road it was, potholes, gravel and boulders in places, with us stopping for sheep crossings and people in the street, and passing horse-drawn wagons of Gypsies, a flashlight held out at the back to warn off oncoming cars.

Jeff was troubled about what to do with the remaining literature we had yet to deliver. If we tried to cross into Soviet territory with it, it would be confiscated, and the team arrested. Yet, it was too valuable a resource to discard. Romanian Christians eagerly awaited its arrival. Finally, we stopped on the highway to hide the black Hefty lawn bags filled with the remaining Bibles in a field thick with towering corn. As usual, each sack was packed with either 150 New Testaments or 100 full-size Bibles, stacked in four columns, forming a cube, then re-wrapped in folded black plastic bags and heavily strapped with packing tape.

Jeff counted on a nearby kilometer marker to lead us to the exact spot on our return journey. He noted the number and went fifty yards into the corn field directly across from it. Because Romanians often walked or rode horse drawn wagons on the highways, every kilometer was marked by a two-foot square concrete post painted with black letters, giving the number of kilometers to the nearest town. Similar concrete markers numbered from one to ten, marked each tenth of a kilometer. Jeff hid the stash, and our two teams left with a prayer, trusting God to keep us and those we served.

We drove through the night, until about 2:00 a.m. Everyone tumbled out of the cars with sleeping bags and slept in a hard damp field for a couple of hours, then, climbed back into the automobiles and resumed our journey.

35

Tangling with the KGB

WE ARRIVED at the Cernovcy border station minutes before the visa stamps expired. Like all Soviet crossings, it was tough, but our teams cleared customs and headed into Ukraine. On the drive to Kiev, a city about eighty miles from Chernobyl, I searched for signs of the devastation and saw none, though I knew they existed.

The six of us checked into a hotel in Kiev. We walked around the town and were almost arrested for witnessing a demonstration in the park. The militia ordered us to leave, and we never learned what it was about. The US is blessed with a liberty that we often take for granted but seeing the lack of it in Communist countries made us appreciate our freedom of worship and speech more than ever.

Later, we drove across the city to Georgi Vin's Baptist church. We listened for hours to the congregants' heartrending testimonies and made notes of their greatest needs. The large sanctuary was painted an airy celestial blue. We enjoyed immensely worshipping there with fellow believers who were the highlight of every journey.

We traveled throughout Ukraine, visiting the homes and churches of persecuted brethren, while filming and documenting their plight. The glowing warmth of these fine Christians who suffered much for the gospel's sake, set our hearts ablaze.

As we visited, it was a privilege to give these precious ones Bibles, food, clothing, and or money, depending upon their needs. They were the saints we yearned to emulate. Many of them were gray and old even in their youth.

Their garments were worn. Yet they possessed a deeply rooted sense of joy and sorrow, which eclipsed much of humanity. Our two teams were simply messengers, honored through the auspices of DOHI to aid them and their causes in some manner, no matter how minuscule.

Often we would pause alongside the highway and prepare coffee. In a restaurant, one might end up with a muddy, lukewarm, caffeine-free concoction. It took mere minutes to set up a table. We heated the water with disposable propane burners that were about four inches in diameter and five inches high. Everyone kept up with their own cups.

About midmorning one day toward the end of our trip, we pulled off the road near a major intersection for a coffee break. While the water heated, everyone studied the maps. A debate ensued on whether to turn left or go straight. Incredibly, the simplest decisions could take on the gravest overtones. The Intourist map showed only one direction to go and that was straight. But Jeff had brought a map from the base which revealed a shortcut. Phil and David swiftly joined him in arguing in favor of the shortcut, which would trim hours off the journey.

I was more than willing to break Soviet law to help fellow believers, but vetoed risking arrest for a convenient shortcut. Tanya and Sonya sided with me, though the men overruled us. We drank our coffee, put everything away and climbed back into the Golf and Toy. Jeff's car took the lead, and I followed reluctantly. Soon we approached a huge intersection. Smartly dressed militia stood in the middle of it, waving small white wands, signaling which way to turn. Jeff tried to go left, but one of the officers blew a shrill whistle and waved his wand, indicating for us to keep straight, which we did. When the militia glanced in the opposite direction, Jeff made a rapid U-turn, with me trailing behind, as both cars whipped right onto the forbidden road.

As I drove, I reflected on how surreal the last few days had seemed—documenting interviews with oppressed and persecuted Soviets—responding to the couriers' many questions as if I knew the answers. A small voice within whispered, "I am only a housewife. I'm not a diplomat or a spy."

Yet there I was in the Toyota, tailing Jeff in the VW Golf, traveling down a questionable section of highway in Ukraine. The last thing I wanted was to get arrested. We journeyed some distance into the rural countryside and gradually relaxed, snapping pictures as we drove.

Throughout Eastern Europe, it was illegal to photograph any objects of a military nature. This included trains, planes, bridges, buildings and even people. Once, in Yugoslavia, two of our couriers were arrested for innocently snapping a picture of a small rural wooden bridge.

Our photos that day had nothing to do with politics. And we weren't US spies, whatever the Soviets might later think. After miles of nothing but dull brown grass to stare at, we were weary. When we blundered into a convoy of military tank transport trucks, trailers and rocket launchers, instinctively all of us started clicking our 35-millimeter cameras. Perhaps we did so, because the sight was novel, and we were bored.

No one appeared to pay us any attention, and we took advantage, shooting as many pictures as possible without actually stopping. A Soviet convoy paused on the side of the road with officers milling around was an unusual sight. We continued down the road with a smidgen of apprehension, discussing what we'd seen.

Reflect on the Cold War, the looming threat of nuclear attack. Try to visualize running smack into about one hundred tank transport trucks, trailers and rocket launchers in the middle of highly sensitive Soviet territory banned to tourists. This might give you a sense of the unease we felt.

We had driven for about an hour and thirty minutes when we came to the next guard shack. Everyone's exuberance fizzled when four vehicles filled with militia surrounded our automobiles and forced us to pull over. A middle-aged beefy officer who appeared to be in charge of the outpost ordered us to get out of the cars, motioning as he spoke to ensure we understood. In a no-nonsense manner, he collected our passports, then radioed headquarters.

Tension slithered and coiled around us like a snakeskin of worry as we waited. Soon a black Volga sedan approached and screeched to a halt. A ranking secret service KGB officer stepped out, confirming we had reason to fear. His steely gaze glinted with purpose, focusing on us for a piercing instant as he walked past.

A myriad of feelings churned within as I watched him consult with the comrade who had ordered our detainment. The KGB officer spoke softly, and in response to his command, the other man whirled and demanded in Russian, "Give me your film."

This was the moment we'd most dreaded. Our first duty was to protect the Christians we had interviewed. Jeff and I, speaking for the group of couriers, shrugged, tripping over ourselves in our rush to explain we didn't understand Russian. Neither of us deemed it necessary to acknowledge that Tanya and David could have easily translated.

Fleshy jowls moving, the officer pretended he was clicking a camera. "Film," he said again and again, growing more irritated at our failure to grasp his meaning.

With a shake of my head I asked, "What is this film?"

Ironically, the Russian word for film is film. Yet we couldn't possibly hand him the pictures we'd taken of believers. The consequences to them could be fatal. Images of the dear faces of those we'd visited ran through my mind, and I prayed as hard as I ever had. Protect them, Lord. Please don't allow them to be hurt because of our actions. Hide the film from these men.

We were encouraged they hadn't discovered the cameras, which were well concealed in the car but far from irretrievable. It was obvious the authorities weren't going to stand for the present stalemate much longer. The atmosphere grew more threatening as harsh staccato orders were fired at us, while we pretended to be in a state of confusion.

Finally, with a brilliance brought on in part by desperation, Jeff queried, "Jeana, do you suppose they're asking for the negatives from our camera?"

Clueless about what he intended, I nodded as if the realization had just dawned on me. "That's probably it."

Jeff gestured to the officers. "Wait. I think I know what you want." He sprinted to the VW and pulled out an old 16-millimeter movie camera, one we had not bothered to use during the entire trip.

Paul must have stuck it in one of the cars, hoping Soviet believers would shoot some documentaries on Christian persecution, which the mission could smuggle out at a later date. This did happen upon occasion although it was a difficult task with the KGB tailing and threatening them. Still, Paul was ever one to cast his bread upon the water to see what it garnered. He hated to throw anything away. The sentiment was a remnant of his youth in Bulgaria as an outcast, with his dad in prison. That day in Ukraine, the old camera was a godsend as the beefy officer seized it and jerked out the film, exposing it to the light. Then he barked, "Into the cars."

I managed a weak smile. "Our passports . . . ?"

"*Nyet.*" He motioned to the militia standing about, and they hustled us into the autos.

A convoy formed, the Toyota and Golf squeezed between two military vehicles, the black sedan following, and another car in front. It appeared the Soviets wanted us out of the restricted areas as quickly as possible to prevent us from observing anything more.

From our place in the middle of the convoy, we raced down the center of the highway, straddling two lanes. A loudspeaker sat atop the first car, and the driver spoke into a microphone, broadcasting warnings for oncoming traffic to move out of the way. The officer in the passenger seat waved a traffic control wand to further alert vehicles traveling in both directions to clear off the road. Automobiles and supply trucks peeled off the asphalt moments before impact, skidding into the ditches. This nerve-wracking odyssey continued for about fifty miles.

171

The convoy halted at the Soviet's divisional military headquarters, a large three-story windowless brick building. The six of us were hauled inside, and then escorted down a dark hall into a small room. The pine paneling on the lower half of the walls made the area shadowy, despite the upper half being encased in glass so the authorities could observe us.

There was a scattering of hard wooden chairs and an old television set with a Soviet war movie running. The sound of machine gun fire blasted from the screen as the Soviets defeated the Americans in ambush after ambush, waging a mental battle against us. We assumed the room was bugged and so we played the part of outraged tourists.

The possibility of them discovering the other cameras and film left us on edge. I knew the Lord was in control. And though I'd securely hidden the addresses and notes from our visits, I found it hard not to second guess myself and God.

The six of us sat there with a variety of thoughts and prayers darting through our minds. The loud staccato rhythm of constant TV warfare had to be ignored if we were to be victors in this psychological war. An officer entered after about forty-five minutes and led Jeff away, reiterating the rest of us were to stay put.

Later Jeff said, "I was taken into the army commandant's office, a big, tough looking woman, who didn't get her position by sitting around and being nice. A KGB plainclothesman and several officers were there as well. They didn't speak English and had difficulty finding a translator. Finally, a Spanish instructor who spoke English was found.

"The KGB man placed a printed confession in front of me. He said, 'You are to sign this at once.' The Spanish teacher translated every word.

"I stared at it, unable to decipher the Cyrillic words filling most of the page. I told him, 'I can't sign this. I have no idea what it says.' The near certainty that they hadn't detected the cameras or film bolstered my courage. Otherwise, I was sure; they would have mentioned it. Their difficulty in finding a translator also encouraged my optimism. I knew the Lord was working on our behalf. And there was the possibility, they were incredibly disorganized and frightened of the Kremlin discovering they had allowed Western tourists into a highly sensitive area.

"The Commandant was in my face, demanding I sign the confession. The KGB man stood on my other side, insisting, 'You have no choice but to obey immediately.'

"I refused. I said, 'Tell me what it says here. You could have me confessing to anything. Besides, I've done nothing wrong.'

"The Commandant sighed harshly and asked me, 'Why were you off the road?'

"'There was no sign warning me not to turn.'

"'You had a mapped route. You were approved to follow it, and nothing else. Yet you turned left.'

"'So I made a mistake and took a wrong turn. Where I come from, they don't arrest people for such things.'

"'Not only do we arrest you, but you must pay a fine as well for breaking the law. First you must sign the confession.'

"They went round and round, pressuring me. I repeated, 'How do I know this is simply a confession that I took a left turn?'

"The KGB man said, 'Enough of this. Sign, at once, or else . . .'

"Hours passed. I realized the equation had to somehow change or we weren't going anywhere. 'I'll tell you what, I'll sign the confession and pay the fine on one condition.'

"'At last,' the Commandant said, pushing the paper closer and handing me a pen.

"'Wait. First, I'd like a letter I can give the consulate at the American Embassy in Moscow. I want the charges clearly spelled out with all the particulars. It must state, there was no sign forbidding the left turn I took.'

"The three stared at one another in consternation and went into a huddle. The chiefs seemed to panic at the thought of word leaking to the Kremlin that we'd been there. They told me to wait and left the room to confer.

"About an hour later they returned looking grim. The commandant said, 'It is not possible, after all, to fine you for violating our travel rules. We cannot give you this paper. We have not the proper form to fine you for the offense. We are dropping all charges.'"

In the meantime, the rest of us were compelled to view more Soviet war movies. We had no idea what was happening to Jeff. Our morale was low. I feared the film had been discovered, and Jeff was in the midst of an interrogation.

Finally, Jeff joined us, and the officer escorting him declared, "Permission to continue with your travel plans has been denied."

Again, we found ourselves in a racing convoy, wincing at oncoming traffic. In each province, the militia would hand us off to a new set of escorts and off we'd go, flying down the middle of the road with a loudspeaker directing all traffic to peel off into the ditches.

We were forced to the border town of Cernovcy and told, "In the morning, you must exit the U.S.S.R. from here."

The authorities brazenly separated Jeff and me from our teams. Despite our protests, they moved us into a bungalow with other Soviets. Jeff and I gazed at each other with the certain knowledge they could have no purpose but to spy on us. We were not home free, yet.

36

In the Corn Fields

JEFF AND I WATCHED as our teammates left for the hotel about one hundred yards away. I envied them the luxury of a third-rate room with a private bath, which probably didn't even have hot water. We stood in front of our assigned bungalow until they were out of sight.

The two of us turned to the officers with a defiance that made no difference. They insisted on pretending we had booked the bungalow rather than rooms at the hotel. Jeff and I had asked to sleep in the mission's pop-up, but the officers forbade it. I disliked sharing intimate quarters with possible spies. I was also disappointed to have the trip suddenly cut short, knowing there were Christians expecting us.

I had every reason to be thankful and praising God. The situation could have ended disastrously but had resulted in the equivalent of a punch on the shoulder. No one had been compromised and nothing of value confiscated. Yet, I was miserable.

The apostle Paul encouraged the early Christians to be content in whatever state they found themselves (Phil 4:11). I longed for such tranquility and dealt with the stress as best I could.

After some discussion, Jeff and I decided to drive into the city to shop. This fit with the image of being tourists, which we wanted to create. In town, plainclothes officers followed us in and out of stores, down the streets, around corners, into the café, through the park and everywhere we went. Our frustration grew. Even the weather seemed to collude with the Soviets as sudden thundershowers drenched us. It was some consolation to see the men tailing us soaked as well.

Back at the bungalow, Jeff parked the Toyota and we stared out at the pouring rain, wondering what we were going to do. Furious at the authorities, Jeff told me what he thought of their methods.

I willed back the tears sliding down my cheeks as I listened to him vent his frustrations.

Jeff glared at me in exasperation. "What are you crying for?"

I gulped back a sob. "For the same reason you're angry," I said hotly, for once seeming to find the right words.

"Oh," he said quietly. A look of comprehension passed between us.

Relief at his empathy burrowed through me as if the sun had peeked over the horizon into our lives. Jeff folded his arms around me, and I savored the warmth of his embrace, holding the knowledge of his understanding close.

Together, we defied the Soviets. When night came, we opened the pop-up in an obscure corner of the hotel parking lot and slept soundly. No one bothered us.

The next morning, both teams loaded up and headed to the Romanian border, where the Soviets forced us to exit. We were anxious to leave the U.S.S.R. The Soviets were equally relieved to be rid of us and swiftly processed us through. We approached Romania, concerned the KGB might have forewarned the *securitate* about us. The customs searches were long but standard. Thankfully, we were permitted to enter Romania. Jeff and I kept a close watch, fearful the KGB might tail us, but saw no signs of this. The farther away we traveled, the higher our spirits soared.

Soon we focused our efforts on retrieving the hidden Bibles we'd left in the Romanian cornfield earlier in the trip. With dismay, we saw the fields were being harvested. Jeff signaled for us to stop. Everyone climbed out of the cars to talk.

So many incredible and out of the ordinary events had occurred that everyone's sense of humor kicked in and soon we were all laughing.

"I can't believe this," I said. "What's next?"

Jeff chuckled. "When I saw those harvesting machines out there, my first thought was, this can't be happening."

David broke in. "What are we going to do if a tractor hits one of those black bags?"

I grimaced. "If it does, they'll shut down the area to search for whoever put them there."

Jeff frowned. "The problem is someone could get hurt. Those books are heavy. If a machine smacks into a block of them—the driver could be thrown."

"Fretting won't help," Phil said, with a lopsided smile. "We're in God's hands."

Jeff nodded. "Let's have a word of prayer, and then we had better get moving."

After prayer, everyone felt better. We got into the vehicles and drove on, carefully reading the kilometer markers along the route for the one that would lead to the Bibles.

A pensive silence settled. Keyed up, we sat on the edge of our seats, asking God, again, to please intervene. At any minute, a tractor could bite into one of the bundles. Images of possible disaster and the subsequent search by the authorities for the instigators pressed in.

My breath caught as I saw we were less than a mile away, and all the cornfields in sight had been harvested. We rounded the bend in the road and spotted our kilometer marker. The reapers had paused for a break right before they reached the field where the Bibles were stashed. How marvelous is our God!

Since there were no public facilities, people commonly walked out among the crops to go to the bathroom. Therefore, it did not strike anyone as unusual for the three men to stroll into the midst of the waist-high corn. They swiftly gathered the bundles and ambled casually back to the cars as if nothing unusual was happening. The guys filled the back of the

Toyota station wagon, then tossed several blankets over the lot, and we were off again.

Next, we had to pass through the scattered militia checkpoints on the route to deliver the Scriptures. An adrenaline rush left us on high alert, and each time we were stopped silent prayers winged heavenward. The officers would collect our passports, and then peer through the windows, matching faces and names. They kicked at the tires and rattled the doors, determining whether a search was warranted. I kept a stash of chocolate bars handy to use as a distraction. "For your children," I would say. This seemed to help. Moments later, they waved us on.

Eventually, we made it to Bucharest and settled at the campground on the outskirts of the city. Later, we were relieved to give the Bibles to our friends, Stefan, a youth minister at the large central Baptist church, and his wife, Carmen. Their joy at receiving them for their congregation more than made up for the difficulties we'd encountered.

Anxious to reach the West, we traveled the entire next day and into the night, hoping to get as far as Hungary. There, everyone could relax their guard a bit. At about 1:00 a.m. we passed through Arad, the last Romanian town before the border. Jeff was in the lead, driving in the Golf with Phil and Sonya as passengers. They were crossing a double set of railroad tracks set rather high, when I heard a loud clunk. The Golf sputtered and died on the tracks. I was following in the Toy with David and Tanya. I stopped and everyone got out to see what had happened. The oil pump and pan had broken.

By then both teams were grubby, hungry and emotionally and mentally exhausted. All we wanted was to go somewhere safe, bathe, eat and sleep. The realization that there wasn't a chance of finding the right parts in Romania hung heavy. The thought of calling the base and waiting for days, while someone brought them down, was discouraging.

Jeff rummaged through the autos and gathered a few bungee cords, which the guys tied together. Thus, we formed a convoy, the Toy towing the Golf, which was in turn pulling the pop-up camper. And that's how we got through the Romanian and Hungarian borders. In both instances, customs passed us quickly through. Neither country wanted the responsibility of a broken-down car with Texas plates.

We stopped at the nearest camping spot and rented bungalows, too tired to even carry in our bags. In the morning, the guys journeyed to Budapest to search for the needed parts. Tanya, Sonya and I stayed behind, resting, washing out a few clothes by hand and drying them in the sun.

Thankfully, the men were able to purchase the oil pump and pan and repair the Golf. Two days later, we arrived in Spittal, relieved to be home again. The couriers at the base had prepared a celebratory feast, and a fun fellowship ensued. Everyone exchanged stories with good humor, praising God for His mighty work. Alex dropped in later to say how glad he was to see us safely returned, and Anita called, happy to hear we had arrived.

Soon the ritual of showers, laundry, trip reports and letters home began. New recruits were arriving, old ones leaving, teams loading and unloading. Happily, in just a few days, we'd be off again on yet another adventure of Godly drama.

THE YEARS SEEMED TO PASS swiftly and God's grace and mercy were with us as we journeyed, smuggling His word and relief to believers while documenting persecution. Some of the more electrifying occasions stand out in our memories. I reflect on them now with a smile at God's handiwork. I'll never forget the incident I wrote about in the prologue. Remember, it happened back in '83. Jeff and I, and two other teams we had pretended not to know were almost at the Soviet border, when a teammate slipped me a minuscule one-by-two-inch tape recorder.

Shelly looked contrite. "Paul asked me to give you this back in Austria and I forgot. I'm so sorry."

Frantically, I peered around the van for a place to hide it. Finding none, I dropped the mini recorder into my purse and prayed it wouldn't be found. In that moment, I didn't feel very courageous, although we'd been smuggling Bibles into Communist countries for a few years.

Earlier that week in Austria, Jeff and I had attended a DOHI board meeting with mission president, Paul Popov. I knew the tapes from the meeting could incriminate us and feared my teammate might have inadvertently handed one of them to me.

The van stopped at the border. The Soviets demanded to see our passports and then initiated the searching procedures that were too familiar for me to feel at ease. They slid under the van to check the undercarriage, took the doors apart and removed the wheels. Jeff went with them to X-ray the tires.

The officers searched our luggage. Finally, one turned to me and said, "Give me your purse."

Terror of what could happen if they found the tape recorder gripped me. Its discovery would expose those in our van, as well as the DOHI teams being searched several parking lanes away.

I struggled to conceal my alarm and handed my purse to the officer as if I had nothing to hide.

He removed my wallet and a packet of tissues and set them aside. Then he grasped the mini-recorder and held it up victoriously. "What's this?"

"A recorder, for music or whatever," I said as if it were nothing important. My prayers spiraled heavenward: Lord, we've been in tight situations many times and escaped miraculously through your grace.

The officer pushed the Play button and Paul Popov's Swedish-accented English rumbled forth.

I felt as if a stray missile had opened a crater beneath me. In a state of shock, I recognized the discussion between Paul and Lee Theodore, which must have been recorded at the board meeting we'd attended.

I pushed back the panic hammering within and tried to behave as if nothing unusual was happening, my SOSes cannoning heavenward. Dear God, how in the world do we get out of this? Please, intervene on our behalf.

Seconds seemed to stretch into minutes. A swift glance revealed nearby couriers who seemed to freeze as they recognized Paul's voice. We avoided one another's gazes, cognizant that a telling look could too easily be intercepted.

Jeff and the guards with our tires had not returned. Instinctively, I wished he were beside me. As I steeled myself for an interrogation, the officer pushed the Stop button and dropped the recorder into my purse, moving on to the next item.

With relief, I realized he couldn't possibly comprehend the significance of the tape because he didn't speak English. I sent a prayer of thanks heavenward. In the natural manner of events, the officer would have called for an English-speaking comrade to interpret. But God in His mercy had moved on our behalf. Praise the Lord!

37

Changing Times

DURING THE REAGAN YEARS, the Soviet's race to keep up with US military strength pushed them into an economic decline, which brought about massive upheaval. One of the miracles attending the political changes of the U.S.S.R. was a new law passed in 1988, allowing visitors to enter with up to twenty Christian books. To test this, Jeff and I, and four DOHI board members traveled on an overnight train from Helsinki to Moscow. We had each packed an assortment of twenty Christian books and Bibles in our luggage.

When the train rolled to a halt at the border, Soviet customs officers boarded and tramped through the passages to inspect the travelers. After years of secret deliveries, it seemed incredible the Bibles were suddenly legal, so our group was naturally nervous. As they entered our compartment, we presented a calm front, relaxed and chatting. We had scattered a few secular novels and magazines about as a diversionary tactic.

The senior agent paused, scanning the room, his gaze seeming to register every detail. "Do you have any other books?" he asked in rigid British English with a strong Russian accent.

We offered what we hoped was a friendly American smile. Jeff and I motioned toward the books lying about.

Without missing a beat, he continued in a demanding voice, "Have you any Bibles or Christian books?"

Our stomachs churning, we nodded and pointed to our bags. One by one, the officials opened the suitcases, tossing the Bibles and books into piles on the compartment beds.

"You can't bring these into the Soviet Union," the senior in charge said, his face flushed with anger. "It's not permitted."

A crowd gathered as more officers arrived and prepared to confiscate the books.

I struggled to swallow the lump in my throat and said, "You can't take those. According to this—" I waved a copy of the Soviet newspaper. "A new Soviet law published in your own press says it's now legal for us to bring Bibles to Christians." I handed him a copy of the newspaper.

A hot debate followed. We declined to give up the literature, and the customs officials refused to allow it through. Curious passengers watched the stalemate in stunned amazement. Few dared to challenge Soviet officials.

Finally, at our insistence, the officers conceded to phone Moscow. After a long tense wait, word arrived; the passage of the literature was approved.

I still remember the excitement, wonder and joy lighting the faces of the faithful Christians who received those Bibles and books. It was like Christmas to them. They could hardly believe the books had been brought into the country legally. One pastor's wife kissed her songbook and then held it close to her heart, tearfully smiling her thanks. Another brother, Sasha, had been arrested and served five years in prison for running an underground printing press which produced the very same Bible dictionary we'd brought him. He was quite moved.

When the Soviet Union's laws later changed to allow the importation of even more Bibles, DOHI couriers once again loaded up. Soviet customs officials marooned in back borders far from Moscow were unaware of the new laws. Interestingly, they sensed the U.S.S.R. was changing and eagerly asked Jeff for details.

38

Doru

INITIALLY, JEFF AND I HAD WORKED predominantly in Bulgaria, Romania, Hungary and Yugoslavia. Later, our travels more often included East Germany, Poland, Czechoslovakia and the Soviet Union. Our German had advanced to a point of sufficiency that caused some of the locals in Spittal to suggest we tackle Kärnten dialect, which to me seemed to have little in common with high German.

For example, the word past, which is *Vergangenheit* in German sounded like *Ah-ya-pasta-shuta* in Kärnten dialect. The obvious Italian influence was from neighboring Italy, a mere thirty-minute drive from Spittal. Since most every county in Austria and Germany spoke a different dialect, its value to us was rather limited.

We decided instead to study Russian, as our trips to the Soviet Union became more frequent. Though people in the East Bloc were required to learn Russian, most disliked it as much as they did their conquerors. Still, we believed it would prove useful.

Jeff and I enjoyed languages and were progressing nicely in the beginning stages of Russian when a setback caused us to refocus our efforts elsewhere.

In Bulgaria, one night as we crept up the steps of a dark housing complex, looking for a contact's apartment, I fell. More frightened by the noise I had made crashing down the hard stone stairs than of any injury, I quickly rose with Jeff's help and moved on before someone reported us. I brushed aside any pain as inconsequential and continued on. In the next few days, the memory of the fall faded, and I marked it down as a small mishap.

When we returned to the base, I headed around the corner to the *Hallenbade's* Olympic-size heated pool to relax the kinks in my back. It was heavenly to swim beneath the towering cathedral ceilings with the glass walls revealing the snow-capped Austrian Alps, perched above the valley of Spittal.

I had the pool mostly to myself, as the Austrians preferred sunbathing by the outdoor pool. A private hedged area separated the two. After a few laps, I winced at the pain in my lower back and then swam faster, thinking to stretch it out. In the next few days, I noticed twinges of pain when I swam but shrugged it aside.

Our next trip took us to Budapest where we met up with Doru Motz and his wife Maria to attend the week-long Billy Graham Crusade. It was phenomenal to have such an event take place in Eastern Europe. Everyone was thrilled and amazed. Many of the pastors we knew from the East Bloc attended. Jeff and I were kept quite busy throughout the conference, networking with old contacts and establishing new ones.

Fortunately, Maria and Doru had the use of a friend's apartment and, since we were all working with DOHI, they kindly invited Jeff and me to stay with them.

Doru and I had first met at the Austrian base. I happened to be there alone when he arrived from the States, demanding a car and money. Most of the courier resources were committed and no one had spoken to me about providing his transportation needs.

"Paul said he would arrange it," Doru insisted.

I glanced at the clock. It was the middle of the night in Los Angeles. "I can't call him now."

At the time, Doru was translating the *Thomas Nelson Open Bible* and *Halley's Handbook* as well as a song and poetry book into Romanian for

DOHI. His father Simeon, a Romanian pastor, was the mission accountant in the Glendale office. Simeon and Jeff were often at loggerheads about funding. Simeon's sympathy lay more with the translators, typesetters and printers than the couriers.

DOHI had published Simeon's autobiography, *The Way of the Cross*, which told the story of his persecution in Romania. Doru's brother, Eugene, who was closer to our age, also worked for the mission overseeing the New Testament Letter Ministry.

I had no idea Doru was coming to the Austrian base until he phoned from the train station in Spittal, asking me to pick him up. In retrospect, I realize I should have immediately confirmed his identity and honored his request.

But then, I hardly knew who Doru was and was protective of the courier budget and resources. I believed they were woefully inadequate, and the translators absorbed a hefty portion of the international budget.

"You've never had to suffer under communism," he said. He seemed to view us as untried novices and to infer the importance of our work was transient. "Most anyone could do what you do."

In the '80s, this tug-of-war between stateside staff and missionaries in the field was tangible. Paul used to say, "I'd like the staff in the States to spend a summer in the field and the couriers to work in Glendale so the two of you could develop an understanding and appreciation of each other's work." Gradually this came to pass, though not soon enough to save Doru and me from an acrimonious afternoon.

He badgered me for a car and funds until I developed a splitting head-ache. In self-defense, I invited him to the Ertl for dinner. During the meal, we reached a compromise, he could have the money, but we couldn't afford to let one of the cars go, with the busy ongoing courier schedule. The summer was fully booked. He could rent an auto or ride the train.

Later, I noticed everyone spoke about Doru with the highest respect. Once, when I visited Buni in Chicago, he mentioned Doru had been by.

I grimaced. "He's rather temperamental, isn't he?"

Buni gave me an unhappy look and assured me Doru was the mildest of men and absolutely brilliant. "You must be thinking of someone else," he said.

I dropped the subject. Paul and everyone who mentioned him seemed to feel the same. Perhaps the afternoon we met was an aberration for both of us.

It was some years later when I next saw Doru at one of DOHI's annual board meetings. We were at a retreat facility on a Swedish island. I hadn't known he would attend. I glanced across the buffet and there he stood. I hoped Doru wasn't going to renounce me there in front of all the board members. Evidently, he felt much the same. He approached me kindly, murmuring an apology for that long-ago afternoon, explaining he hadn't quite been himself. I said something of a similar nature to excuse myself.

Doru was there to provide an update on the progress of the *Romanian Open Bible Study Bible* translation, and Jeff and I were to report on the courier ministry.

In our presentation to the board, we included two video clips Jeff had shot. One was of Rodica Cocar, the head secretary of the Baptist Union, in her Bucharest apartment. She was also Benjamin and Buni's cousin. Her brother Daniel was a pastor as was her father Mircu. A smiling willowy figure, she had long dark brown hair and eyes that gleamed with humor and intelligence. Rodica had opened her home and heart to us repeatedly. In the video, she held an open poetry book in her lap, which Doru had translated and the mission had published. Romanian Christians especially cherished this version. Rodica sang one of the poems, in her pure operatic voice. It was hauntingly beautiful.

Jeff had shot the second film earlier in the summer at the Oradea campground. We were there in the white van rendezvousing with couriers in the Diamond. It became clear, the young people parked next to us were also Bible smugglers, though our teams never spoke with them. They were such a perfect example of what not to do that Jeff, hidden from their view inside and behind the mirror film on our van windows, shot some scenes for DOHI training seminars.

To begin with, the young people glanced nervously around the campground, their anxiety reflected in their eyes. They then disappeared into their camper and drew the shades. Shortly thereafter, they began piling disassembled tables, couches and miscellaneous objects on the ground outside. Next, they went inside, apparently to take the compartments apart. The camper rocked and the area echoed with the banging of hammers and the buzz of drills. Back outside, one of the men drove a van close to the camper. The group of untrained couriers carried boxes out of the camper and loaded them into the van.

Then they all stood next to the pile of furniture and fearfully watched two of the men drive away in the van. Before they returned the items inside, the couriers formed a circle and prayed. We prayed for them too because they obviously had not been well trained. It was no wonder about twenty-five RVs a summer were confiscated at the Romanian border alone.

While showing this film clip to the board, we pointed out the errors this young group made and went into detail regarding DOHI training methods. We also showed slides of some of the Christians with whom we worked. Then we gave an involved update, with handouts and budget projections of the Austrian base operations.

Doru and the rest of the board seemed impressed. His report impacted us as well. Best of all, through the years we'd grown to appreciate each other's work. Jeff and I had the privilege of delivering the first newly published shipments of the mission's Romanian translation of the *Halley's Handbook*. Pastors were thrilled to have the first commentary ever in their own language.

Many clasped it to their chests, exclaiming their gratitude with comments such as, "Thank you. Thank you. This is better than gold. Such a treasure. You can't imagine what this means to us."

I witnessed the respect these pastors had for Doru, both as an individual and a translator. Truly, the afternoon we met must have been an off one for both of us.

Doru had seen many couriers come and go, some doing more harm than good, while through the years our commitment had only grown. We too had seen staff come and go. Doru's father and brother had left to begin their own mission. Also, the network of friends and contacts we had developed and supplied were many of Doru's colleagues. Later, at the board meeting, Jeff was elected international VP. And for Doru and us, a sense of mutual appreciation and respect had evolved.

So, when we attended Billy Graham's Crusade in Budapest and shared living quarters, we were quite at ease. The event was perhaps one of the earliest signs of the changes soon to come in the East Bloc.

Looking back, I realize I shouldn't have shrugged off my back pain. If I would have only grasped that period was but a portent ushering in monumental changes in my life as well.

39

God's Grace

DURING THAT STAY in Budapest, intense lower back pain awakened me early each morning, but I continued to ignore it. At the conclusion of the Billy Graham Crusade, Jeff and I bid old and new friends *auf Wiedersehen* and drove to the Austrian base for a brief respite.

A six-week journey followed. Toward its end, we rendezvoused at a hilly, crowded campground in Prague with couriers Joanne and Bob and Ted and Shirley who were driving RVs. The couples unloaded the literature they'd brought for us to deliver.

The next several days, we distributed the coveted children's literature and also met with contacts to explore the possibility of Door of Hope International enlarging its *Open Bible Study Bible* translation projects to include a Czech version. Historical changes on the horizon, however, were soon to affect DOHI in a manner that made this impossible.

One evening, Joanne, Shirley and I set out for a brisk hour walk, the pain in my back significantly hindering my enjoyment. Despite my attempts to brush it aside, it was growing worse. We hiked through the camp, relaxing our guard and chatting with ease. None of us had stayed at the campground before, and it was pleasant being unknown.

Joanne taught high school German and Spanish in Michigan, and her husband Bob was a dedicated NASCAR fan in his off time. They were cheerful regulars we depended on and capable team leaders, as were Ted and Shirley.

Shirley, a tall redhead from Jackson, Mississippi, was married to Ted, a banker. Ted often invited, "Kathryn, why don't you and Phillip come on in and sleep in the camper with us instead of the pop-up?"

"No thank you." Without any hesitation, I backpedaled from his suggestion. There might be running water, a kitchen and bathroom in the RV but having once spent the night in the same room as Ted, we weren't anxious to repeat the experience.

Though a marvelous person, he snored like an out of control locomotive roaring down the tracks. When we had driven them back to the base after the fifth wheel was confiscated, circumstances forced us to share an accommodation in Hungary. I don't think Jeff and I slept any, because Ted snored so loudly. We began to understand why Shirley's gaze frequently held a tired, sleepy look.

Couriers who returned annually to the mission field lived in close quarters. They also shared deep experiences and common goals year after year. Like a family, we teased and laughed about each other's shortcomings while admiring the strengths we had come to rely on.

One afternoon, a summer volunteer had offered free haircuts to the couriers. She could be wicked with a pair of scissors. John ended up with a crooked, partial burr cut, long before they came back into fashion. He viewed the results and thanked her, a huge, sincere smile lighting his face.

The rest of us grinned. Who else besides John would thank someone with so much joy for creating such a mess? I've seen him work in the garage until eight at night, loading compartments, and then rush inside to help his wife with dinner. We were grateful for the extraordinary couriers God provided. This thought was uppermost in my mind as Shirley, Joanne and I walked.

Soon we'd completed our mission there and with no wish to linger in Czechoslovakia, we returned to Austria and wrapped up the summer's work.

In the fall of 1989, a tour of the Soviet Union loomed ahead with twenty-seven US pastors, and some of their wives, booked to accompany us. Jeff had arranged for an official tour and an extra nice forty-passenger bus and driver.

The Soviets had recently passed yet another law stipulating there was now no limit on the number of Bibles that could be declared and brought into the country legally. Thousands of Russian New Testaments were ready to load onto the bus to test the new law.

Brother Sunny, who worked with Milldale, a Baptist press located in Zachary, Louisiana, was to be on board as well. Milldale Press had also shipped sixty thousand Bibles to be picked up when our group arrived in Leningrad. These failed to surface on the trip, but hopefully, they traced them later.

Jeff also arranged for Margaret Nicole to translate as he led the group into Soviet Christian homes and churches. Margaret, a Bulgarian, was fond of telling us how she and Paul had played together as children. When she married, Margaret followed her husband to East Germany. An accomplished violinist, she went on to become concert master and first chair violin with the Dresden Philharmonic. She later defected to the US and came to work for DOHI, playing her violin and speaking on behalf of the mission.

Margaret was an exuberant statuesque blonde with a smile that seemed to stretch and touch everyone. She drove a red sports car. At each meeting, she gave her testimony and concluded by playing the violin. It was quite moving. I'd helped book her first tour of Texas and arranged for her to stay with Jeff's parents. She fell in love with The Woodlands.

Ironically, a Texas pastor she met on DOHI's Soviet tour had started his own mission and offered her a position, making it possible for her to move to Texas. We bumped into each other occasionally and Margaret's same bubbly enthusiasm always engulfed me. Sadly, she recently passed away. The harvest of souls in fields grown high with needs cries out for more laborers in Christian missions.

In the fall when the group departed on the Soviet tour, I remained in

Austria, too ill to travel. This was a groundbreaking trip. I was sad to miss it. Unfortunately, as we prepared to leave, the ache in my back became excruciating. At night while Jeff slept, I paced the floor, praying for relief.

As Jeff and the group departed for the U.S.S.R., I waved goodbye, hiding my disappointment. It seemed my attempts to learn Russian were in vain. The base was closed for the winter and everyone gone but me.

I visited my friend Anita's family physician who gave me injections of cortisone, which had no effect. Next, I consulted with Dr. Oblau, an elder in Alex's church, who was chief orthopedic surgeon at the larger hospital in Klagenfurt, but found no answers.

Frightened, not knowing what was happening to me, and exhausted from lack of sleep, I agonized about what to do. I was miserable, whether lying or sitting. Even walking hurt. The weight of a small section of the newspaper was too much for me to hold and the effort sent my entire body into spasms. My back couldn't tolerate the eleven-hour flight home. Austria's medical system was like a web of foreign code seemingly impossible to crack.

At our apartment one afternoon, discouraged and hurting, I phoned Anita and asked, "Can you drop by for a visit?" I avoided telling her on the phone that Jeff was gone. We had to carefully consider every word we said in case the lines were bugged.

Anita had no idea my back was still debilitated, and went on to talk about the theater and parties keeping her busy. "I would like to visit but we're going dancing later. You understand. Bye-bye, *auf Wiedersehen*."

Alone, I indulged in a light meal of self-pity and tears. Daniel, from Belgium, rang to discuss some mission business. Afterward, I set the phone back in its cradle, a little heartened by the human contact.

My gaze fell on our address book, a red three-ring binder with about eight hundred entries, neatly printed from a database Jeff had created. I thought of all those within, family, friends and business associates from around the world. Who could I turn to in my time of need?

I flipped to A and saw Dilly Andersen on the first page. I knew without a doubt I could ring her, and she'd do everything possible to encourage or help me. I didn't call Dilly but was immensely comforted knowing I could.

Slowly, I went through the directory name by name, reminded of numerous others who cared. That exercise blessed me. I didn't need to phone anyone. God had already lifted my heart and He was right by my side.

By God's grace, I met the chief orthopedic surgeon at the hospital in Spittal. He ordered X-rays and diagnosed the problem as Spondyloysthesis, a degenerative separation of the lower fifth vertebra. The doctor gave me a series of injections up and down my back to numb it so I could travel home. Reluctantly, he repeated the process when the first procedure failed to bring relief.

Jeff returned in time to see me off and to tell me all about his trip. When their tour group initially approached the Soviet border, custom officials motioned them from the bus, collected their passports and queried in Russian, "Do you have anything to declare?"

Margaret, the team translator, turned away slightly and said in a low voice, "Twenty thousand Bibles."

"What?" the officer asked, unable to hear her clearly.

"We have twenty-thousand Bibles to declare," she said loud enough for all to hear.

The Soviets nodded to everyone and said, "Welcome to the U.S.S.R."

It was amazing to witness *perestroika* and *glasnost* in action and watch it spread across Eastern Europe. Everyone on board the bus was affected. A number of new missions sprang from that tour, such as Bibles for Russia, a successful venture started by Alfred and Jean McCroskey. Yet another of the Baptist ministers aboard expanded his operations to include Siberia and other parts of the Soviet Union that were difficult to reach.

Naturally, the Soviets required one of their own be included to serve as a guide. They chose a history teacher who was upset at shepherding a group of Christians. Eventually, she loosened up and confided how difficult it had been for her to deal with the changes in her country. The history books she taught from were being rewritten.

I was happy to hear how the Lord had blessed their trip.

Jeff drove me to the airport. It would be six weeks before he could join me. Our plane tickets, purchased originally for an around the world flight, were valid as long as we flew in an easterly direction. We hadn't planned on flying direct to Houston because of fall speaking engagements in Europe and Australia. Thus, we had the added cost of airfare to the States for my treatment and then the return to Europe in order to use the fare we'd purchased.

Several days before my departure, I had managed to catch a severe head cold. Thank goodness I boarded the KLM flight to Houston with a large enough supply of cough drops and Kleenex to get me through the trip. My head felt like mush, and my back was numb. I pitied the poor men who sat on either side of me and hoped they didn't catch my cold.

When I arrived home, I visited Dr. Crockett, who verified the Austrian doctor's diagnosis and prescribed physical rehab, medication and rest. To sit was still extremely painful. He advised me to walk around a bit after every twenty minutes of sitting, which wasn't easy to do while traveling.

In early December of 1989, Jeff and I were faced with a thirty-one-hour flight to Melbourne. DOHI's director in Australia had booked us months in advance for three weeks of meetings, which we were committed to attend. I dreaded the flight.

Money was tight and the US economy was in a downswing. We lived on a nominal salary from the mission and deputation, which paid our plane fares. DOHI covered other travel costs and provided lodging and food while we were in Europe. The trip home for both of us had been an unavoidable extra expense. It would have been lovely to fly to Melbourne direct if we hadn't already purchased special around-the-world fares.

God had every care for us. When we reached Amsterdam, KLM apologized for overbooking coach and bumped us up to business class. Words can't express what a blessing this was in my condition. I thank the Lord to this day for His infinite provision in every situation.

Some might say this was a coincidence, but God's divine intervention in our lives has long been apparent to Jeff and me. He called us to Him when we were deeply lost, and with coal-black dust polished these souls into something He could use.

40

Australia

ON THE TWENTY-ONE-HOUR FLIGHT from Amsterdam to Melbourne, we enjoyed forty-five-minute reprieves in Malaysia and Singapore. The price of English books at these airports precluded me buying any, but our stock of Bodie Thoene's *Chronicles of Zion* novels kept us enthralled. When the KLM 747 finally landed in Australia, we were met by a smiling pastor from Uganda who pastored a church in Melbourne.

We piled into his small car and traveled about a mile before he pulled off the freeway due to a flat tire. He had no spare. In a sense, it was deja vu, as we added Melbourne to the list of cities in which we'd found ourselves broken down.

Jet lagged, all I wanted to do was sleep. Instead, we sat on the grass while the pastor walked to find a phone and call his wife for help. Thankfully, we were soon happily settled in his charming home. Jeff and I spent a lovely week there getting to know some of the Christians and speaking at different churches. Everyone was warm and kind. Since most of the services we spoke at were in the evenings, our days were often free. We enjoyed touring the wildlife sanctuaries and gardens in the December summer sunshine.

At the end of the week, we flew to Sydney where Jeff and I met Kathy, DOHI's Australian director, and she outlined the rest of our itinerary. "I've booked you in Brisbane this week and Sydney the following one. We'll leave tomorrow on the afternoon bus and arrive in the morning."

"Jeana and I already have airline tickets to Brisbane and back. So there's no need for a long bus ride," Jeff said.

"I bought bus tickets for the three of us," Kathy insisted with a firmness that was hard to combat, as we were her guests.

The ensuing seventeen-hour bus drive across the plains was harrowing. The driver zoomed down a cross-country, two-lane highway. We prayed the entire night as he fearlessly maintained his speed and crept repeatedly into the adjacent lane of oncoming traffic to pass slower cars and trucks. Thank God, our group arrived safely, but two other buses on the same route that evening collided, killing the passengers.

Brisbane was a large, bustling city on the Gold Coast, and the Australians greeted us with open friendliness. Their accents, food and customs such as driving on the left side of the road seemed very British. Some of the congregations we addressed were quite large. To break the ice, I usually shared how petrified I was on our first Bible smuggling trip and how God miraculously ensured the Bibles passed safely through the border. Jeff ran the projector while I talked the audiences through a brief visual, highlighting the mission and the needs of those we served.

Jeff followed with a message on how God was moving in the courier ministry. He included Scriptures and our experiences. Our intent was to alert Christians to the plight of their brothers and sisters in bondage. These meetings invariably increased donations to DOHI and enlarged its mailing lists. This resulted in an increase in funding for the courier ministry. We were generously received and found most people had a sincere desire to help those less fortunate than themselves. Australian Christian radio interviewed us as well.

To our surprise, we learned a growing population of East European immigrants resided there. We stayed with a Czechoslovakian family and supped with Soviets. Those we met lived in large, new brick homes the government had provided as part of a settlement when they arrived.

Before we left, Jeff and I wanted a night to ourselves on the Gold Coast. So, one evening after services we made the short drive to a waterfront motel we'd reserved. We dined at a quaint candle-lit Mexican restaurant serving Aussie-style enchiladas.

In the morning, the two of us strolled hand in hand, our bare feet digging into the honey-colored beach. A strong, prevailing wind blew hair and sand in our eyes. We basked in the sun's warmth, splashing through shallow turbulent waves that knocked us to our knees. We came up gasping at the strength of the surf.

Later, Jeff and I strolled along the wharf, licking cones of frozen yogurt swirled with icy chips of banana and pineapple. We caught up with Kathy toward the end of the day and offered to pay her plane fare to Sydney. In light of the earlier bus trip, she gladly agreed to fly but wanted to buy her own ticket.

Much of the Australian architecture reminded me of the US in the '50s and '60s—one-story homes and store fronts with flat roofs. Sydney, though, was quite cosmopolitan. Jeff and I lodged with a Soviet family there whose background was similar to DOHI staffers like Kathy, her sister Val, and Ruth and Ted. Like thousands of others, their families had fled the U.S.S.R., escaping into China, for a time, until persecution again sent them fleeing to Australia. Many settled there. Some moved on to Canada or the United States where, today, large Russian-speaking congregations exist. The believers we stayed with served a lot of ethnic Chinese meals, recreated from their years spent in China.

Jeff and I delighted in exploring Sydney. Since our days were mostly free, we toured several breathtaking Japanese gardens, attended the magnificent shell-like Sydney Opera with its phenomenal acoustics and rode the ferry to nearby islands.

From Australia, we flew to Hawaii for a week's vacation, a perk of the around-the-world fare. The two of us stayed in a modest hotel with a kitchenette near the beach. I happened to be reading a brochure in our room and discovered a car rental for a dollar a day was included. Amazingly, we had this comfy place to stay and a new car rental for only $51 a day!

We drove around the island, discovering glorious isolated beaches with lighthouses, and coconut trees swaying in the breeze. It was Christmas week and the high tourist season rolled into one. And as heavenly as it was, after a few days we longed to be home with family. Jeff and I had been traveling almost nonstop since April, and the leisure time hung heavy on our hands.

Our friends Tim and Rosamma attended Youth with A Mission's University in Kona between stints of serving as missionaries in India. We flew to the island and enjoyed a marvelous fellowship. They, too, were homesick and especially glad to see us. They drove us to the National Volcanic Park. I was astounded to learn the visitors' center had disappeared beneath the encroaching lava six months earlier. If ever there was a hint of what hell was going to be like, it was there. Still, we found it fascinating.

Jeff and I returned to Waikiki. Weary of vacationing and travel, we called the airlines and booked an earlier flight. The five-hour flight to Los Angeles on Christmas day was almost empty.

We were to attend the US board meeting there. Ruth and Ted (DOHI's Russian language typesetters) were nice enough to interrupt their holiday, meet us at the airport and take us home with them a few days early.

Usually, it was Hiro's job to transport staff. A kind Armenian, he was short and stocky, with a smile that flashed a mouthful of gold teeth and lit his face. He worked in the mission mail room, but his driving always left me on edge. Los Angeles traffic was enough to do that on its own.

Hiro, like many of his fellow Armenians, had immigrated to the States from Armenia. His daughter Takoosh, her husband Haik and their family lived in Tehran, Iran. Those of us who knew Hiro were horrified in

1994, to learn his son-in-law, Haik, had been brutally beaten and stabbed to death by Iranian authorities. A few weeks before his death, Haik had visited with Paul Popov at DOHI's Glendale office. He asked Paul to come to Iran to help train and prepare pastors and Christian leaders for the more severe persecution he believed was imminent. But Haik deserves a chapter all his own.

41

Bishop Haik Hovespian Mehr

MORE THAN TWO THOUSAND Iranian Christians of all denominations gathered in the bitter cold to bury Haik and stand with his wife and four children as they watched the casket of the father and husband they loved lowered into the ground.

A true contemporary Christian martyr, Haik was also the late general superintendent of the Assemblies of God (AOG) Churches of Iran. His persecution didn't begin on the day he was murdered. For years, he traveled extensively, establishing and supervising AOG's Iranian churches. He dared to openly express the needs of his fellow brethren and speak out against their persecution to government authorities. Muslim officials repeatedly threatened Haik regarding his evangelistic work.

At his funeral, an official spokesman for Iranian church leaders said, "We do not know who killed him, but this we know, that he died for his faith and for his firm Christian stand. Therefore the church in Iran considers Bishop Haik Hovsepian-Mehr to be a Christian martyr."

A Catholic priest with tears streaming down his face began to shovel earth over the coffin. "This man is a saint and a martyr," he said.

Despite a difficult childhood and a struggle to complete his schooling, Haik gave his heart to the Lord at the age of fifteen and started ministering when he was seventeen years old. In 1967 he married Takoosh Markosian. Two years later, on their way to church, Haik and Takoosh were seriously injured in an automobile accident and lost their six-month-old baby.

After their recovery, despite trying conditions, Haik pastored in Gorgan for fourteen years, preaching the gospel to Armenians and Muslim Iranians. In 1981 he accepted the position of general superintendent and transferred to Tehran where he was later elected bishop and went on to become leader of all the AOG Churches in the Middle East. Haik also served as Chairman of the Council of Protestant Ministers in Iran. Like the Apostle Paul, he gave his life for Christ.

Shortly before his death, Haik mobilized human rights efforts on behalf of his friend Rev. Mehdi Dibaj, a converted Muslim who had been imprisoned for nine years. He focused international attention on Dibaj, who was to be executed in January 1994 for his conversion to Christianity. Suddenly, without explanation, Dibaj was released from prison on January 16, 1994.

Three days later, Haik vanished on the way to pick up his sister-in-law from the airport. Although his family notified area police stations and other security offices of his disappearance, they were not informed of his murder until twelve days later. Iranian authorities said police discovered his body in one of the suburbs of Tehran. He had been stabbed several times in the chest. Despite the two sets of identification Haik carried, police were unable to identify his corpse.

They buried him in an Islamic cemetery outside of Tehran without telling the family. They showed the family photos for identification, which revealed signs of torture. By request, the family received his body for Christian burial, but authorities allowed them to view his face only.

The AOG headquarters in Springfield, Missouri, reported that in early January, Haik had called and said, "If we die or go to jail for our faith, we want the whole Christian world to know what is happening."

Haik had many chances to immigrate to the West but chose to honor the work God had called him to do. Because he was an ethnic Armenian born to Christian parents, under Muslim law today, his abduction and murder were illegal and unjustifiable. For a converted Muslim such as Dibaj, the law is different. Haik's wife and their four children were left without the protection of husband and father in a nation adverse to Christianity. Haik's two brothers, who also pastored churches in Iran, remained there as well, despite grave danger.

Paul Popov had met with senators and members of the US State Department on behalf of the Hovsepian-Mehrs. Those of us at Door of Hope International felt deeply for Hiro and his daughter Takoosh and her children, and mourned Haik's death.

Our longtime coworker and friend, Ivette Moradian, was Paul's assistant and DOHI's general office manager. She also attended Iran's Philadelphia Church where she became a born-again Christian before she immigrated to America. Ivette has a unique sensitivity and burden for those forced to endure oppression and persecution. She said, "I can relate to those in other countries who have been hurt or killed for their faith. My ethnic background is Armenian, from Iran, and we as a people have always endured tough times."

Every week, news of Christian persecution filters into DOHI offices from Eastern Europe, the Middle East, Central Asia, and Asian Communist countries. The faith of these believers has set them apart from others and left them at odds with governments unwilling to tolerate any variations in points of view. In the mission's California office, for decades Ivette has handled correspondence, accounting and received requests for aid as well as reports of new baptisms and Christian oppression. She is also the mission's field director for Iranian ministries.

She has been a dear friend through the years and maintained a firm belief in the mission's purpose. "Door of Hope International provides relief," she said. "People in tough times rely on outside assistance. We provide that. But we're not just foreigners coming in, giving aid, and then leaving. Everything the mission does is through the local churches. They are the vessels we use. We don't make ourselves too big, too known. We ask the believers what they need and then we try to supply it.

"Anyone can go in to assist a Christian in another country who is in trouble. But do they have the background, the training? We know the cultures and have the connections. And we have the experience."

Ivette has served with DOHI for more than forty years. Her husband Vahi has always supported her mission work. Her close association with the ongoing struggles of believers worldwide has given her a rare perspective on Christian faith. There have been times she has phoned and asked us to pray and fast, because the mission income was dropping and the persecuted pastors' relief salaries, Bible translators and printers had to be paid.

Her gentle, sweet spirit, strength and intelligence integrate into one lovely person, her faith expressed in every breath. "I don't see Christianity as an easy life. You pay a price," she said. "Those sharing Christ's torture will enjoy the fruit of His glory. Christians who are persecuted these days can identify with the saints in the Bible who were also persecuted for being followers of Christ. They went through that, is what you think when you hear about believers' troubles. That's part of Christianity."

DOHI's international offices have long been a connecting point where Christians in the West can touch base with pastors and believers in countries where the mission is at work. Ivette, especially, has a heart for those suffering under harsh Muslim regimes. Because of our experiences in Eastern Europe, Jeff and I carry a deep burden for the plight of oppressed and persecuted believers living under communism. The truth is that Christians continue to suffer under both Communist and Muslim regimes. Many are murdered for their faith.

In 2002, 63,000 Christians were trapped in the Indonesian province of Maluku, an area where for decades they'd lived peaceably with neighboring Muslims. This was before extremist Muslims poured in to bolster the militant Jihad warriors already there. Their forces destroyed thirty villages and four thousand homes. Though numerous fled, many were killed. Most of these innocent believers were defenseless farmers and fishermen who had no choice but to remain.

Before armed Muslim extremists poured into the area, the Christian population of Maluku was 40.5 percent. Such religious cleansing has displaced hundreds of thousands of Christians in Indonesia and destroyed hundreds of churches.

In 2003, an estimated 194,000 Christians were martyred around the world. There are more martyrs now than there were in 100 AD during the Roman Empire's persecution of believers. The numbers continue to rise. In 2017, more than 250 million Christians suffered persecution or death for their faith. The fight for religious freedom is costly. The families of those who've given their lives to preach the gospel or to worship with their children or neighbors in North Korea and like places have learned this in the most painful manner possible. With today's technology and access to information on the internet, it is easier than ever before for Christians and churches around the world to mobilize and help pressure governments to protect the rights of fellow believers.

Jeff and I made the decision years ago to lend our voices to this great chorus of believers. I'll never forget the promise I made to God one Sunday morning at a church in Varna, a Bulgarian coastal city on the Black Sea. I remember lifting my bowed head from where I knelt praying on the dirt floor. I saw tears on the worn, gentle faces of the women and men in the crowded service. They shed tears of joy that they had not been forgotten. Someone in America had cared enough to send us across the ocean with Bibles and relief assistance. The gift of knowing they were not alone in their suffering and persecution brought them great comfort.

As they hugged me and whispered their heartfelt appreciation, I promised the Lord to never hesitate to speak on behalf of these precious Christians. I often reflect on how God had placed Queen Esther in a position to influence the King to save the Jews when evil was plotted against them, and thus they were spared.

Hebrews 13:3 admonishes us, "Remember those who are in bonds or persecuted for Christ's sake as though bound with them." We have been blessed to live in the United States of America, a country of wealth and power, not by accident, but because God ordained it. And I firmly believe God has placed Jeff and me here for a reason too.

42

Coming Home

OUR FLIGHT FROM HAWAII landed in Los Angeles on Christmas Day, 1989. Instead of disturbing Hiro, we phoned Ted and Ruth to pick us up. They were close to our age and a couple with whom we shared a common purpose. They welcomed us warmly and Ted made us delicious Russian perogies from scratch. The couple had left their home in Canada and moved to Burbank to typeset the *Russian Open Bible Study Bible*. At the time, DOHI still used linotype rather than PCs for such tasks.

Later during the US board meeting, Paul formally asked us to relocate to Los Angeles. We regretfully declined. With my back still in a vulnerable condition, we chose not to add to our current responsibilities.

In January, we flew home to Texas. Shortly thereafter, we began receiving calls from Door of Hope International asking us to reconsider our decision. Paul was taking a year's sabbatical, and the mission wanted Jeff to serve as de facto president in the interim. After Jeff and I prayed and came to better understand the need, we agreed. The mission paid our moving costs and provided an adequate housing allowance. With my added health problems, a comfortable place was uppermost in our minds, especially after living in tents and traveling for months on end.

We found a lovely apartment in Burbank convenient to the office. It was also near enough to both Paul and Agneta, and Ruth and Ted, for us to easily fellowship. Paul offered the use of Haralan's furniture, which had been in storage since his death. Back in Conroe, our pastor and his wife and their two children were staying in our home while theirs was being built. Hence, our transfer went forward with ease.

Weekends usually found us with Ruth and Ted, who were also transplants, and Paul and Agneta and their children, with whom we had enjoyed several past vacations. A nine-to-five job seemed liberating after our relentless overseas schedule, though conferences and meetings frequently ran into off hours.

Ivette became even more dear as the three of us drew closer in our efforts to keep the mission running smoothly. She was often the glue that helped hold the US office together. When Margaret wasn't on the road, she was engaged in translating a hymn book soon to be published in Bulgarian. She shared an office with an assistant who booked her itineraries.

The Glendale, California, DOHI family then included Developmental Director Mark Duzik and Eugene Motz who headed the New Testament Letter Ministry, Frank Schwenden who oversaw the mainframe computer system, Artoosh and Trajan who ran the print shop. Dr. Kim Strutt, a Presbyterian minister and a DOHI US board member with a doctorate in filmmaking from Fuller Seminary, acted as consultant. His wife Julie was receptionist. Raymond Logan contracted the artwork and Joel McCallum handled the direct mail fund-raising appeals and magazines. These are some of the staff with whom we worked.

Our tasks were varied. We continued to stay in touch with East European contacts and provide updates to the necessary sources. I remember applying for the copyright for the *Romanian Open Bible Study Bible* and negotiating with Thomas Nelson to purchase the rights to use their maps for the Study Bibles.

One afternoon, while I was on the phone with an out-of-state ministry representative, the building began to shake. Everyone was ordered to evacuate. Foolishly, I couldn't bring myself to say, "I've got to go. There's an earthquake." I concluded our conversation and joined the staff outside, but by then the six-point quake had passed.

One evening, I received a phone call from one of Haralan's grandsons. He and a friend needed to furnish an apartment they had rented. After we talked a few moments, he said, "Paul suggested I call and see if it would be okay if we dropped by and picked up a few of Grandfather's things."

"Yes," was the only possible answer to such a question. He and his friend came and bit by bit took everything but our bed, which we had newly purchased. It started with an end table, then a chair and sofa, next a chest and the dining table and on and on. After a while, I slipped into the bathroom, locked the door and sobbed quietly.

I knew it didn't matter whether we had a chair to sit on or a table at which to eat. Yet, my heart seemed to crumble with hurt. Our lives were so unsettled. We had an apartment in Burbank, another in Spittal and a home in Conroe. The friction of dealing with inner politics and factions within the mission was wearing. I also dealt with continual back pain. In the mornings, I drank my coffee while pacing because sitting was too painful. Jeff and I still traveled extensively. The woman in me wanted to fashion a familiar and safe nest, yet God was compelling me to look to Him for my security and to trust Him to provide.

I could hear Jeff calling in the background, "Jeana, where are you?" Embarrassed, I tried to stifle my tears.

He knocked at the door. "Are you in there, Jeana? Let me in."

Hurriedly, I splashed water on my face, dried it and unlocked the door.

He could see I was upset and wanted to know why. Finally, I confessed, then whispered, "Please, don't tell anyone else."

He hugged me. "If it means that much to you, we'll buy some furniture."

My tangled thoughts spilled out, tears sliding down my cheeks again. "We don't have enough money. And I shouldn't care about such things."

"It's all right," Jeff said, stroking my hair. "We can find used items in the paper."

How could I be sad with such a wonderful husband? I summoned a smile and went and chatted with the two nice young men until it was time to say goodbye. The rest of the week, I took off work and chased down ads in the paper. I drove to University, Hollywood, Ventura, Santa Monica and further in my search, dragging Jeff with me in the evenings.

For $945, I furnished the living room, dining room and bedroom. This included a Thomasville pecan dining set, two beautiful walnut secretaries, an elegant Italian provincial sofa, end tables and two upholstered chairs and a chest of drawers.

Jeff and I entertained office staff and European directors occasionally at our apartment. Elisabeth from France, Phil from England and others visited or stayed. Thanks to the Lord's grace, we always had a pleasant place for them. Once again, God had uniquely blessed us beyond our needs.

The year in Los Angeles was perhaps the busiest yet. For convenience's sake, we hosted the annual courier training seminar there and put off leaving for Europe as late as possible in order to have more time to attend to business at the home office. Some of the board suggested we forego the trip. Jeff and I had a heavy schedule and our regular influx of couriers planned. Our responsibilities at headquarters, though, caused us to end the courier season a bit earlier and return to Los Angeles.

Each day brought new challenges. Jeff coordinated varied Bible projects and helped supervise the organization's intricate functions. With the opening of the Soviet Union, many major nonprofits that had not previously toiled in Eastern Europe kicked off ministries there with huge stateside radio and TV advertising campaigns. DOHI could not possibly compete. Its funds were already overcommitted to the three ongoing Russian, Romanian and Bulgarian *Open Bible* projects, pastor relief and like areas.

For more than a decade, DOHI's *Open Bible* translators had painstakingly labored, translating reference and study materials for the *Open Bible* and typesetting the text, producing the first new Russian language Bible plates in one hundred years. In the Romanian and Bulgarian versions, archaic language and spelling in the original text were updated as well.

It was a period of testing and change amid political tensions as well as jubilant rejoicing with Christian friends in Eastern Europe. Paul, still grieving the death of his father, struggled with God's vision for the future, questioning whether the mission's commission had been fulfilled with the opening of the Iron Curtain and the growing new religious freedoms there. After a period of thought and prayer, he emerged with a stronger vision, placing a greater emphasis on reaching lost youth. Under his leadership, Door of Hope International went on to establish soup kitchens, orphanages, schools, summer camps and evangelical ministries to orphans and homeless street children as well as prison outreaches across the former East Bloc and in the Middle East.

Paul never forgot the anguish his family experienced when the Communists arrested his father. He was five years old then, and twenty when he next saw his dad. He also never forgot the food packages and Christmas toys that arrived from Christians in the West during those thirteen long years and five months his dad was imprisoned for his faith. Thankful for the prayers, which brought his family through that terrible period, Paul knew firsthand the yearning and hunger of those deprived of Bibles and freedom.

Again and again, Jeff and I witnessed the great need for Bibles in Communist countries. In one instance, a DOHI missionary at a Soviet crusade handed an older lady a Bible. She exclaimed with tears in her eyes, "Lord Jesus! For sixty years I have prayed for a Bible of my own. I knew someday You would give me one. Thank you! Thank you! Thank you!" Through the years Jeff and I have been privileged to witness, time and time again, such tears of joy from believers.

The mission's emphasis on translation and printing God's Word continues. Door of Hope International also reaches out to thousands of children, orphaned and homeless, living on the streets without parents or guidance, as well as those placed in juvenile prisons, often for merely stealing bread to survive.

After the Berlin Wall fell in 1989, dramatically changing history, DOHI immediately set up offices in Eastern Europe. In Bulgaria, The

Haralan Popov Foundation was established. Jeff and I realized it was time to return to our home and family in Texas. Our work with the mission continued from there.

In the past, Jeff and I had often been called upon to document persecution and write in various venues. I became managing editor for the *Door of Hope International Magazine* as well as the US communications director, writing and editing the monthly appeals and a variety of ministry publications. For more than a decade, I served in this capacity. I have since worked in DOHI's publishing arena as both an editor and writer. I have been privileged to oversee two revisions of *Tortured For His Faith* (2005 and 2018) and the revision of *The Fugitive* (2020) and a revision of the soon to be published story of Ruth Popov's life, *The Book of Ruth*.

My last trip into Eastern Europe was in 1993. Jeff and I drove from Romania to Bulgaria, crossing into Serbia during the Bosnian war. About fifty kilometers from the fighting, we drove with the gauge on empty, praying for fuel, when there was none to buy because of the war embargo. God miraculously saw us through in the manner He always has. What a great God we serve!

When we reflect on those years, Jeff and I are grateful for the tens of thousands of Bibles and related Christian books, which passed through the Iron Curtain to the beleaguered Christians who so desperately needed them. Despite the hard work and danger, it was extremely satisfying to work in this particular vineyard of the Kingdom.

Our memories about the difficulties of those perilous years—often living in primitive, uncomfortable conditions, separated from family and friends and the comforts of the American way of life—may fade. But we'll never forget the joy of obeying God in His covert work, the appreciation of those receiving the Bibles we brought, and the assurance that Christianity behind the Iron Curtain was nurtured by our actions.

Appendix

Scripture References for Battling Fear:

Matthew 1:20, 10:28, 14:26, 21:26
Mark 4:41, 5:33
Luke 12:5, 32, 19:21, 21:26
John 7:13
Acts 10:22
Romans 8:15, 11:20, 13:7
1 Corinthians 2:3
2 Corinthians 7:5, 11:3
Ephesians 6:5
2 Timothy 1:7
Hebrews 2:15, 12:28, 13:6
1 John 4:18
Jude 1:2

Made in the USA
Columbia, SC
25 June 2021